Anthony C. Winkler was born in Kingston, Jamaica, in 1942. He was educated at Mt. Alvernia Academy and at Cornwall College, both in Montego Bay; at Citrus College in Glendora, California; and at California State University in Los Angeles. He is the author or co-author of many college textbooks on rhetoric and English Grammar that are widely used in American colleges and universities. His first novel, *The Painted Canoe*, published in 1984 to critical acclaim. This was followed by the *The Lunatic* (1987), *The Great Yacht Race* (1992), *Going Home to Teach* (1995), and *The Duppy* (1997). A short story collection, *The Annihilation of Fish and Other Stories*, was published in 2004 by Macmillan. He has also written two movies: *The Lunatic* (1991) and *The Annihilation of Fish* (1999). *The Burglary*, a play, was produced in Kingston, Jamaica, in 2001 and in Toronto in 2005. Another play, *The Hippopotamus Card*, was produced in 2005 by the German radio station WDR under the title *Das Rhinozerossystem*. He resides with his wife, Cathy, in Atlanta, Georgia, USA.

THE ANTHONY C. WINKLER COLLECTION

The Lunatic

Anthony C. Winkler

MACMILLAN
CARIBBEAN

Macmillan Education
Between Towns Road, Oxford, OX4 3PP
A division of Macmillan Publishers Limited
Companies and representatives throughout the world

www.macmillan-caribbean.com

ISBN-13: 978-1-4050-6881-9
ISBN-10: 1-4050-6881-7

First published by LMH Publishing Ltd, Jamaica 1987

This edition published by Macmillan Publishers Ltd 2006

Typeset by Newgen Imaging Systems (P) Ltd., Chennai, India
Cover design by Gary Fielder
Cover illustration by Judy Ann Macmillan

Printed and bound in China

2010 2009 2008 2007 2006
10 9 8 7 6 5 4 3

Introduction to Macmillan Edition

Many people, on first reading *The Lunatic*, think it was an easy book to write. But every book is hard to write in its own unique way. In the case of *The Lunatic*, the storyline unwinds on the very edge of preposterousness and the difference between a humourous episode and one that threatens to plunge the narrative into absurdity often turned out to be a mere word or phrase or two. There were many times when I went over the material incessantly, trying to make a certain episode work. When I was successful in fixing a troubled paragraph, I would often be amazed at how a passage that just a moment ago seemed dead or dense suddenly sprang humourously, even hilariously, to life.

Of all the books I've written, *The Lunatic* has been the most satisfying in terms of feedback from readers. What has surprised me most was the number of cancer patients who told me that reading *The Lunatic* made them laugh so hard that it helped them get through chemotherapy or endure postoperative pain. I did not write a novel meaning to do that. But I'm glad that *The Lunatic* has had that effect on some seriously ill people.

As a freelance writer who writes for his supper, I seldom have time to work exclusively on fiction written on spec. Most of my time is spent between projects that pay in money and projects that pay in pleasure but have no certain buyer. In the case of *The Lunatic*, I alternated it with a textbook on computers that I was writing with an academic in Virginia. My mornings were devoted to writing about computers, and my afternoons to writing *The Lunatic*, which took more than a year to complete. I opened the story with the lunatic prancing about in the village commons, taking as my model a local madman who spent many hours of his day in the public market, harassing buyers and sellers alike. After that, the engine that drives the narrative is the humour, and the humour is derived mainly from turning things on their heads. In my fiction, I often invert things to see how they look upside down. So instead of Jamaican men preying on tourist women, a lusty tourist woman is intent on sexually devouring as many Jamaican men as she can.

The initial response to *The Lunatic* in my immediate family was disappointing. In the normal course of things, when I'm finished with a project I bounce it off my wife to see if she likes it. I do not know anyone in my life who is more supportive of my work than my wife, and she's especially gentle with me because having lived with a writer for thirty years, she understands about easily bruised egos. But it was plain to me from her mystified reaction and silence that she didn't like the story. Coincidentally, my mother was over on her annual visit, and she asked if she could read the manuscript next. But unlike my wife, my mother is merciless with any literary unconventionality, and for the next few days she walked around toting the manuscript and reading it in snatches to periodic eruptions of "What a fool-fool book!" or "How man can talk to tree?" "Tony, you don't see you write a stupid book?" Her reaction was especially troubling because as a Jamaican, she would have instantly got any Jamaican nuances that my American wife might have missed. But whether or not she got them, she made it clear that she hated the book and thought it rubbish. I was in despair.

I do not know what might have happened after that if fate had not intervened. But a neighbour of ours who was also an avid reader, overhearing my mother, my wife and me squabbling about my latest manuscript, said to me, "Let me read it, Tony, and I'll give you an honest opinion." So I gave it to her, and she disappeared with it in the afternoon and showed up bright and early the next morning. She'd had a fight last night with her husband, she said, that ended up with him throwing a shoe at her. The reason for the fight? She'd been reading the manuscript and laughing so loud that she woke him up and sent him into a rage. "I think this is going to do it for you," was her parting comment.

It was on the strength of her reaction that I sent the manuscript of the novel to my Jamaican publisher, who greeted it ecstatically. My neighbour was right. *The Lunatic* is probably my best-known book. A reviewer in the *Washington Post* called it "the funniest novel" he had read in years. Out of gratitude, I dedicated *The Lunatic* to my neighbour, Katharine Harper.

Writing a novel is a little like birthing a child. There is a kind of agony to both acts along with an exultation of creation that is nearly inexpressible. Criticism is especially wounding as the baby painfully emerges, and the last thing the one in labour needs to hear is something like, "What an ugly baby!" Over the years I've learned to let a manuscript sit for a while before I show it to anyone, and to never show work in progress to anyone, except God.

The Lunatic is still not my wife's favourite, but she has contributed to it. My working title had been *The Place Beneath*, from Shakespeare. But it still struck me as too enigmatic. We were discussing my dissatisfaction with the title one evening when she suggested offhandedly, "Why not just call it *The Lunatic?*"

I took her advice; the rest, as they say, is history.

BOOK I

Chapter One

There was a road in the mountainous countryside and there was a ragged black madman dancing on it. On both sides of the road the land unfolded in waves of pastureland dotted with groves and marked by the dips and hollows of dried-up gullies and streams. The surrounding fields were green and lovely to look at, but it was to the antics of the solitary madman that the eye was involuntarily drawn. Sometimes he would leap up and down in one spot until he was too tired to jump anymore. Then he would start off down the road on an erratic course, weaving from side to side like a drunken pedestrian. And sometimes he would shriek like a child at play, and in the very next breath he would moan like an old man under a heavy load.

Exhausted with his antics and dancing, the madman rested beside a cut-stone wall. He was panting and blowing hard for breath when suddenly he heard a noise. Since talking cows sometimes sneaked up on him, and giant birds, and beasts that defied description, the lunatic quickly ducked behind the wall to see what or who now stalked him.

He heard a scratching sound first, which made him draw a sharp breath and hold it. Then he saw a woman coming out of the bush.

She was a woman from the village on the brow of the mountain, and she was taking the shortcut through the bushland on her way to market, a heavy basket of yams swaying on her head. But now that she had come to the cut-stone wall marking the path of the road, she placed the heavy basket on the ground and blew with exertion like a winded donkey.

Glancing furtively about her, she lifted up her dress, peeled off her panties with one deft motion, and began pissing from an upright position.

The madman bounded from behind the wall with a howl of outrage.

"Jesus God Almighty!" the woman screamed.

"No wee-wee before me eye!" the madman bawled, covering his eyes and turning his head.

Recognizing the village lunatic, the woman shrieked, "Aloysius! You make me wet up me shoe, you damn brute! What you hide behind de wall for? Look what you make me do to me shoe!"

"Me no want see no pum-pum loosen water before me eye!" the madman sobbed.

She spread her legs implacably wider and continued her pissing while the lunatic turned his head away and screamed at her to stop.

When she was done she tore off a branch from a bush and wiped her legs. Then she hoisted the basket on her head, climbed over the wall, and set off down the road.

"Damn nasty negar woman!" the madman shrieked after her. "Why you come wee-wee in de bush. Woman supposed to wee-wee in a toilet, damn nasty negar woman!"

"Go 'way, you mad brute!" the woman yelled scornfully, without turning her head to look back at him.

The madman walked over to the puddle the woman had made on the ground and he took some cut stones off the wall and threw them on it. He scuffed dirt over the stones with his calloused bare feet until he had covered the dark patch her water had made in the earth.

"No come show me no pum-pum dat loosen water before me eye!" he screamed one more time.

"Hush up, mad brute!" came the faint derisive reply from far down the road.

Down the asphalt road that flowed through the green fields and between the undulating banks of two cut-stone walls, the woman trudged under the heavy basket of yams, and she cursed this damn country, this blasted Jamaica, a country where a decent woman could not even stop in the bush to catch a piss in peace without being terrified into wetting her own legs by some raving lunatic jumping out from behind a wall and carrying on like a Minister Without Portfolio. "Go 'way," she screeched crossly at the top of her lungs, for her feet were bawling about the hot sun on the hard road, and her belly crying for a cold drink, and her aching shoulders wondering why they had ever been born, just like an American teenager.

Yet she had not understood the ravings of this lunatic Aloysius, who now clambered through the thicket and who from a distance she might have mistaken for a grotesque and enormous black bird, his hair being matted and dirty, his appearance woefully shredded by life in the bushland.

For all his unkempt and wild looks he was still a man, and to a man a pum-pum is like a bone to a hungry dog. It is a thing a man will dream about even if he is hungry and sick. He cannot help himself, for Almighty God put pum-pum between the legs of women and then he put dreams about it into the heads of men, even into the head of a lunatic.

Every day Aloysius saw women in the village and smelled their rich black and brown bodies and stared as they wriggled past him, their pum-pums hidden under calico frocks and pink panties, guarded by watchful constables, suspicious boyfriends and bad dogs. But all he had done for years was look at women and dream. Because he was known by everyone in the village to be a homeless lunatic, all the pum-pum in the parish was closed to him. No woman would permit him to put to her the feverish arguments that man is born to put to woman. And now this impertinent pum-pum, the first he'd seen in years, had the nerve to callously wee-wee right under his nose and then saunter away with a basket of yams on its head as though he were a stone or a bush and not a man starving for a woman.

What he had just witnessed, this lunatic was telling himself sorrowfully, was just such a sight as could shock a man into madness, and as he walked through the bush he fought to control his emotions.

"De woman was rude and out of order!" the lunatic screamed suddenly and fiercely to a lignum vitae tree.

Out of order: a parliamentary phrase that Milud and Milady of the fallen British Empire might use to scold one another at Whitehall. Yet after three hundred years of colonialism by the ancestors of Milud and Milady, it is a phrase that Jamaicans of all walks of life use to signify outrage, indecency, impropriety – even a woeful madman such as this Aloysius.

Chapter Two

Aloysius Hobson was the proper name of this madman. But when the madness was raging inside him, he claimed to have a thousand names that he bellowed out on the street corners for all the world to hear. Around him the villagers thought it unsafe to even whisper the word "name" for fear he would overhear and begin ranting and raving his bogus names in the voice of the madhouse.

Last year one of the villagers had had an elderly aunt from America staying with her, and this relative fell into conversation with Aloysius on the street and asked him his name, and the lunatic immediately began to spout: "Aloysius Gossamer Longshoreman Technocracy Predominate Involuted Enraptured Parliamentarian Patriarch Verdure Emulative Perihelion Dichotomy Intellectual Chaste Iron-Curtain Linkage Colonialistic Dilapidated ..."

Believing this to be some bizarre form of village humour, the woman interrupted with a hollow laugh and the harmless remark, "How can anybody name 'Longshoreman'?" which drew an indignant cry from the lunatic and a ferocious onslaught of, "Impracticable Loquacious Predilection Abomination Vichyssoise Pyrrhic Mountebank Unconscionable Altercation Lookalike Partition Bosky Pigeon-toed Dentition ..."

A crowd gathered quickly in the village street to witness the antics of the ranting madman, who had pinned the aunt by the wrists to prevent her from running away before he could recite his entire name.

The aunt was struggling in the grip of the raving Aloysius, the crowd was swirling restlessly at its edges, poised between taunting the madman and fleeing from him, when the village constable hurried over to quell the disturbance.

"He won't let go!" the aunt screamed, wriggling in the grip of the lunatic.

"Aloysius!" the constable barked. "Aloysius, what you name?"

The lunatic turned his fierce glare on the constable.

"Me say," he croaked, "me name Aloysius Gossamer Longshoreman Technocracy Predominate Involuted Enraptured …"

"How dat go again?" the constable asked, prying the lunatic's fingers off the wrists of the struggling, terrified aunt. "Start from the beginning, I think I miss one."

"Listen! Clean out your ears!" Aloysius shrieked.

"My fault," the constable said gently, freeing the aunt. "I hard o'hearing. Start from de beginning."

Pried free, the terrified aunt ran sobbing towards her niece's house while the lunatic began his chant once again, "Me say, me name is Aloysius Gossamer Longshoreman Technocracy Predominate …" to the delight of the gleeful crowd.

"Too much blasted noise in de street," the constable interrupted again, "too many inquisitive people. Start from de beginning and come wid me down to de station house where me can hear you whole name."

The madman paused in mid-recital, a glowering look of suspicion clouding his black face.

"Station house? You say station house?"

"Yes, so me can hear you whole name," the constable explained, putting on a most reasonable air.

"All right," Aloysius assented. "Make we go."

But as soon as the constable started to elbow his way through the surrounding throng, Aloysius bolted in the other direction and ran through the village street shrieking, "Aloysius Gossamer Longshoreman Technocracy Predominate Involuted Enraptured Parliamentarian Patriarch Verdure ..."

All stood in their tracks and watched the madman streak past the market and disappear into the bush.

"Boy, me could never catch him," the constable said, making a sucking sound of finality through his teeth. "Me belly too full wid de mackerel and green banana me eat fe breakfast."

How did this lunatic who could not read learn so many words? Some he had learned in the streets of Ocho Rios from the Rastafarians, the men of the beard who smoked the ganja weed and dreamed of going back to Africa.

These Rastafarians, who called themselves the brethren, were a good source of words, even if they disapproved of pork eating, for they were avid Bible-readers and had learned many words to describe Africa. On the street corners of Ocho Rios, while a sleek white tourist ship sat contentedly in the harbour preening itself like a fat swan, Aloysius would sit among the brethren, smoking the weed with them and listening to the words they used for Africa.

It was a place of great beauty, the brethren said, this Africa, this motherland they yearned for like a foundling for its natural mother. The black man belonged to that gentle country – he had sprung from its soil; the waters of its rivers and streams ran through his veins. When the brethren spoke about Africa, they were the sons of a rich father longing for Christmas.

Listening to the brethren dreaming about their lost homeland taught Aloysius many new words that became a part of his name.

But most of the words he knew and took as his name Aloysius had learned from the new brown-skinned teacher at the village school. She was a young woman from the parish of Clarendon who walked through the village with her nose in the air saying nothing to the villagers except "Good morning," or "Good afternoon," or "Good night," when she passed them in the streets.

This stuck-up teacher was also a great one for reading. Late at night the villagers would see the yellow stain of light from a kerosene lantern against her curtained window. During the daytime hours, she walked through the village streets with an unabridged dictionary between the crook of her arm like a fat chicken. At recess, when the children were playing boisterously in the school yard, she sat by herself under a tree and read.

Now the government admitted that the schools were overcrowded and classes were too large and facilities were bad, but in the very next breath the government always said that there was no money for improvement and that every teacher must try to do his best with what little was available.

In the case of this school teacher, her class of fifty-five students was held in a common room along with five other classes, with only a blackboard positioned between them. The old teachers knew that the only way to teach in such an overcrowded and noisy room was to have the students recite their lessons in unison. So when one class was learning geography, the students could be heard chanting, "The capital of St. James is Montego Bay; the capital of St. Catherine is Spanish Town; the capital of Westmoreland is Sav-La-Mar." And in the arithmetic class only a thin blackboard away, another fifty students would also be chorusing, "Twice one is two, Twice two is four, Twice three is six, Twice four is eight, Twice five is ten," and next to these, another fifty students might

be reciting important dates in the life of a foreigner named
Columbus.

The school was often so noisy from all this continuous
reciting that even far way in the bush the children's voices
would carry to the ear of the labouring villager as a faintly
cacophonous buzz of facts and multiplication and dates, and
his heart would swell with pride to think that his child was
among the learners bleating these fundamental truths.

But this vain new teacher taught her children little
geography and only the occasional multiplication table. Mainly
she taught them words, words, and more words. Nothing galled
this teacher more than to reflect on the wicked unfairness of
vocabulary. Why should a white Englishman be able to say
about a dog that it was "docile" while the children of a poor
black Jamaican could only mutter that it was "tame"? If he
chose to be boastful about it, the Englishman could even add
about the dog that it was "compliant, pliable, tractable,
submissive, amenable" and "yielding." "Tame, Tame, and more
tame" was all the poor tormented black children could reply.
What was fair about that? What was just about a white man
having twenty names for a tame dog while a poor black child
had only one? Which bank would be willing to entrust
responsibility to a negar clerk who could call a tame dog by
only one name?

But to her children the dog would be everything the
Englishman could say plus another five or ten words more. Other
children in the school might have a "pain," but hers suffered
"anguish, paroxysm, throe, distress, pang, twinge" and "woe."
During daylight hours she caused her students to bawl out
definitions of words with such authority that the learned chanteys
of the neighbouring children were drowned out under bellowings
of: "Idiomatic – in accordance with the individual nature of a

language" or "Nascent – coming into being; being born" or "Famulus – an assistant, especially of a medieval scholar."

When Aloysius found out what this new teacher was doing, he began hiding under the window nearest to her class and would crouch there listening to and repeating the words chanted by the children. Here he picked up: "Gossamer – a filmy cobweb floating in the air or spread on bushes or grass" and "Technocracy – government by technicians, specifically, the theory or doctrine of a proposed system of government in which all economic resources, and hence the entire social system, would be controlled by scientists and engineers." Here he learned most of his thousand names.

But one day the teacher spotted him outside the window and marched immediately to the principal.

"What is this?" she asked indignantly. "Now I must teach lunatics too?"

Alarmed, the principal jumped up from his chair.

"One of your children has gone mad!" he cried in anguish. "I knew it! Too much blessed vocabulary! I told you you can't come in here and teach the whole blessed Oxford dictionary to country children."

"I'm talking about a genuine lunatic," the teacher said frostily, "who is lurking under my windowsill. He hides there every day."

The principle ducked out the door and returned in a moment looking vastly relieved.

"Oh," he shrugged. "That's only Aloysius. He doesn't trouble anybody."

"I refuse to teach vocabulary to a lunatic. He must move from under my window."

"Listen, Miss Williams," the principal said earnestly, "you're new here. Believe me, I know the ways of these people. One .

harmless madman under a window doesn't trouble anybody. Why make a fuss?"

"I don't care if is one madman or fifty. It's the principle of the thing. I am not going to teach vocabulary to a lunatic, sir."

"Lawd, Miss Williams," the principal pleaded, lapsing into a little sociable patois, "ease up a little, nuh? He's just a harmless fellow. He likes to hear the lessons."

"Mr Raffety," she hissed, "vocabulary is not for lunatics."

So Aloysius was forced from the school. At first he resisted. He argued with the principal and he even flew into a rage and screamed out two hundred of his names for all the school children to hear. But then the constable came and chased him into the bush and when Aloysius returned the next day, hoping to sneak back under the window, he found that the principal had tied a bad dog to that side of the school building. Being afraid of dogs, Aloysius was forced to stand far away from the window while the animal looked him in the eye and bared its teeth and the children taunted him with the new words the teacher had taught them: "Dementia – Loss or impairment of mental powers due to insanity;" "Berserk – In or into a state of violent or destructive rage or frenzy;" "Run amok – To rush about in a frenzy."

Later in the week, Aloysius spotted the teacher in the village and crossed the street intending to beg her to let him return and listen to her lessons, but she saw him coming and took the big book from out between the crook of her arm and held it grimly between her fingers and stared stonily at him, which caused him to quail on the far side of the street.

Yet by then he had learned a thousand names, and when the madness struck him, he recited them to the awed villagers in a voice heavy and hoarse and gravelly – a voice he got from being homeless and sleeping out too often in the cold bush.

Chapter Three

Aloysius lived in St. Ann, a big-boned parish of mountains and foothills rolling down to the sea. It is a parish of heavy rains and wild vegetation. Tree grapples tree for room in the sun. Perched high on limbs like carrion birds, parasite plants suck life and sap from everything that grows. Wild vines and lianas ooze menacingly out of the dark earth to seize and entwine the trunks of towering hardwoods.

In this wilderness near the village of Moneague Aloysius now tramped, looking for something to eat. He beat his way through the bush, emerged into a clearing planted with guinea grass, and searched for the calaban he had set this morning.

The calaban was a bird trap made of mesh-wire moulded into a rectangular shape and baited with wild berries. When the bird tried to eat the berries, its feet tripped a string causing the cage to fall and trap it.

Once in a while he would find a bird in the calaban. Usually it would be a small bird such as the grass tit or yellow breast – a bird so scrawny that picked and cooked down it resembled a parboiled lizard. But even a scrawny bird could be juicy and flavourful when boiled with wild pepper. He could sit beside a fire and suck on the bones of the bird and daydream that he was eating chicken.

Aloysius suddenly remembered that he had hidden the calaban under a naseberry tree, and he walked across the clearing until he was close to the tree, then he got down on all fours and cautiously stalked through the grass to see if there was a bird in the trap. He was nosing his way past a tussock of guinea grass when he glimpsed the trap. It was empty.

He stood up, dusted off his rags, and peered around him. He saw nothing but the bare and empty land stripped like a bone in the breeze. His belly began to growl.

Before the night could catch him in the open land, he hurried to the place in the bush where he kept his pot and where he had left behind a small piece of cooked yam.

Because Aloysius had no house or hut but wandered fretfully from place to place, often sleeping in the open, the pot that he used should have been anywhere in the bush. But one lonesome night when he had been wandering through the dark bushland, picking his way by starlight, he had come upon a towering flame heart tree, and he had rested against its trunk and the wind had soughed through its limbs and the tree had spoken respectfully to him like an old friend. So from that night on he settled under this tree, and made a ring of small stones on which he kept the kerosene can that served as his pot. Here he built his fire every night, cooked his supper, and slept on a litter of crocus bags.

He found the stale piece of yam and sat down among the charred stones where he usually lit his nightly fire and ate it.

When he was done his belly still groaned its ugly song of hunger and a restless worm gnawed his insides with the hard gums of a toothless infant.

He stared up at the darkening sky and wished that tonight the sky would rain a loaf of bread or a fish as God had once made it do.

"Rain a fish, beg you," he said to the sky.

"Rain fish?" An unseen bush sneered. "You think God Almighty going put fisherman out of work just to fill you greedy belly?"

Aloysius glared around to see which bush was mocking him. But they all stood like grim and darkened dwarfs in the twilight.

"Me hungry!" he bawled out to the empty bushland.

His voice echoed across the silent shrubs and the conspiratorial copses of trees watching him in the falling darkness.

"Sorry, Aloysius," the flame heart tree said with sympathy. "Me wish me had a fish to give you."

"Get a job," a bush hissed spitefully. "Madman must work for a living like everybody else."

If it were not so late he could have found fruit to eat. Naseberries and mangoes and sweetsops grew wild nearby. But he did not like to walk alone at night in the bush for he was terrified of meeting strangers in the darkness.

Chapter Four

It was a long night, a hard night. Sometime before midnight a patou appeared in the trees and began to hoot, and this sound so frightened Aloysius that he sat up and stoked the fire and peered timidly into the black night held at bay by the flickering flames.

When he slept out in the bush he did his best to avoid cattle, for he had found them sneaky, insomniac, and given to windy digressions. He would not sleep near a herd of goats, for they were lecherous tellers of nasty jokes in the pitch black of the night – a time when Aloysius always tried to think pure thoughts to ward off nightmares about death. He also preferred to sleep in a spot where there were no bushes but only large trees. If you overlooked the ghoulish appearance that darkness gave them, trees were by far the best company. Some were sympathetic; some would murmur and rustle and whisper; others might speak a word or two every now and again, but if he said something polite such as, "Listen, Mr. Tamarind tree, me want sleep now," the tree would invariably murmur an apologetic "Pardon," and be still.

It was just the reverse with a bush. Bushes were born babblers; bushes talked about cricket matches and old spin bowlers, about old movies such as *Scaramouche*, and old movie stars such as Stewart Granger or Richard Widmark; bushes never knew when to shut up and could not take a hint that the time had come for sleep. You could bark at a talkative bush, "Hush you damn mouth!," and the bush would reply with a sour proverb and keep on babbling as much as ever. Aloysius had no use whatsoever for a bush.

After midnight, after the patou and the muttering of a few distant bushes, after the immense night settled over the fields with the fire gnawing raggedly at its edges, the dew began to fall. It fell like a rain, because of the elevation of this country, and it fell so heavily that even though Aloysius was sleeping against the trunk of the leafy flame heart tree he still felt damp and uncomfortable.

He moved nearer the fire but was afraid that a spark would ignite the crocus bags, so he moved back under the tree where the dew beaded over his bare face, causing dollops to roll off the end of his nose.

Nevertheless, he fell asleep. The ground was hard and the bushes of the fields were babbling in a distant murmur, but eventually he fell asleep.

And he had a terrible, wicked dream. There was fire in it, and water, and an unseen beast that lurked in the belly of a deep, sniggering shadow. And there was another force, too, something he could feel but not see, that pushed him inexorably towards the laughing shadow. The lunatic struggled against the force, which locked him in a wrestling grip like a pugnacious constable, then he awoke suddenly, screaming at the top of his lungs.

The fire flickered weakly; the stars were fading. Across the eastern sky a paleness seeped slowly from the rim of the mountain, settling over the earth and sky like a mist.

In the distance a bush was lamenting over some dreadful news. The lunatic craned to listen.

"God Almighty," the bush was bawling, "Collie Smith dead and bury him in him prime!"

Old news. That was the way bushes were: they grieved over old news, stale, worthless news. Collie Smith – a young man, a cricketer of great promise cut down in the flower of his youth in a terrible car accident – dead and buried over twenty years now, and here a foolish bush in the wild was just bawling over it.

Aloysius was in no mood for stupid keening this early in the morning.

"Hush you mouth, you rass bush!" he screamed. "Or I goin' come and chop you down wid me machete."

A dead silence fell over the countryside.

Suddenly Aloysius was aware of two men staring somberly at him in the dim light. He shrieked with terror and clawed for his machete.

"Good morning, Aloysius," one of the men cried hastily.

His heart pounding, the lunatic peered through the dusty morning light and recognized the two villagers on their way to work on the land.

"Blood!" Aloysius screeched at them, his heart still thumping with fear. "What de rass you sneak up on me for?"

"Sorry, sah," said the other, the older one, gently. "We just taking de footpath down to Busha's pasture."

"Damn rass people!" Aloysius fumed. "Is not enough dat de damn bush bawling 'bout Collie Smith, now de two of you sneak up on me like duppy, and me just wake up! What de rass wrong wid you?"

"Say what? Who bawling 'bout what?" the younger man asked cautiously.

"De rass bush! Him just hear 'bout Collie Smith so him must deafen me ears wid him bawling! Bush always hear bad news last. Me just tell him to hush his rass mouth or I going chop him down."

"Oh," the older man said glumly. "Jamaica bush always chat too much."

"Is true, you know," the younger one echoed. "Nobody is a bigger chatterbox dan a bush."

"Good morning, Aloysius," the men murmured respectfully, moving off slowly down the footpath, vanishing in the waterish glow of dawn that was settling like an enormous tangled cobweb over the slumbering fields and valleys.

So now that the dawn was here his belly was bawling out again, but he had got nothing to feed it. The yam was cold in his belly; the day stretched before him long and hot and empty.

He washed his face in a small spring that bubbled out of the ground. He found a chewstick tree and snapped off a twig and chewed it to remove the taste of night from his mouth.

For the next hour he foraged through the bushland, picking wild naseberries and sweetsops and eating them. When he was full he sat against the bole of a tree and tried to remember what he was to do today.

But today, as was usually the case, he couldn't remember. His brain liked to play tricks on him. Sometimes it was clear and sharp and he could remember even the smallest details of his childhood. But other times everything was foggy and unclear, and he could hardly remember from one moment to the next. When his brain got that way, Aloysius found that the best thing for him to do was to act as though it didn't matter to him whether or not he remembered. Usually if he pretended that he didn't care, his brain would work properly and he would remember what he was supposed to do.

He took his machete and started off across the bushland, heading for the road. But as he was passing a scruffy bush, one that stood off in a corner by itself like a thief, he paused and eyed it savagely.

"You!" he addressed the bush, slapping it with the side of his machete. "Learn dis now. Collie Smith dead dese twenty years. I don't want to hear no bawling 'bout it tonight, you hear me, Mr. Rass? Or I going chop you down right now!"

"Sorry," the bush mumbled.

"Sorry, Mr. Aloysius! Sah!"

"Sorry, Mr. Aloysius. Sah," repeated the bush.

"A-hoa," Aloysius grunted triumphantly, giving the bush his grimmest look.

"What me name?" he asked the bush again.

"Mr. Aloysius, sah," the bush replied timidly.

Every man liked a little respect; every man liked to hear "Mister" before his name, and "sah" after it. Aloysius stood there for a moment, savouring the respect, looking for a little more.

"Lord Aloysius," he finally declared, with a sniff.

The bush balked.

"Dere is only one Almighty Lord," it said huffily.

The lunatic raised the machete as though he would cut the bush into two pieces with one stroke, but then he paused and reflected that the bush was right, that it was going too far to ask anyone to call anyone else Lord anything. So in spite of himself, he had to admire the bush for standing up for right principle.

"Dat's right, Bush," Aloysius said grudgingly. "Me was just testing you."

"Thank you, Mr. Aloysius," the bush replied.

"A-hoa," Aloysius said with satisfaction, heading across the clearing for the road that led to the village.

Bushes, like unruly schoolboys, needed to be occasionally reminded of their place in the world.

Chapter Five

The path Aloysius took to the village was roundabout and crooked. He wandered from one side of the road to another, swapping taunts with schoolboys, pausing to chat with old men airing themselves before the gates of tiny houses, screeching loud good mornings to housewives who glowered at him over their brooms from dark doorways. And because he was Aloysius Hobson he exchanged words not only with people filing into the village through the footpaths that criss-cross the bushland, but also with cows, dogs, donkeys, and even the odd bush or two – all clamouring to press their opinions upon him. In his wake he left a chorus of gloomy villagers, a sea of gravely shaking heads, a sprinkling of oaths against the government for allowing such an obvious madman to roam the streets as freely as a stray goat.

If Aloysius was aware of the consternation he left in his trail he gave no sign of it. One moment he would be bawling out a word or two from his thousand names, and the next he would be frantically attempting to speechify a little pum-pum out of women he met on the road. Most of them brushed him off with a contemptuous stare; a few laughed scornfully; one or two picked up stones and threatened to crown him if he came too near.

Yet he did meet one woman, and she encouraged him so in his speechifying that his heart began to beat faster with hope that at last he might get a little pum-pum. She was an ugly old crone – her body stringy and bony, her head nearly bald, her neck as shrivelled as a chicken's. In her mouth a single snaggle-tooth rose like a crooked mangrove in a sea of black gums. Aloysius helped her with her basket of fruit, which she was carrying to market, and walked alongside her telling her jokes.

When he was able to shut out the cries of nearby bushes he was very good at telling jokes. This morning he was in such good form that the old woman had been cackling steadily over his monologue as they walked. He told her jokes and watched her slyly out of the corner of his eye, and all was progressing well between them when suddenly he heard a growl, "You not goin' ride me!"

Where had it come from? Aloysius looked around nervously.

"Who say dat?" he asked out loud.

"Me! Me, de pum-pum say dat! Me say dat you not goin' ride dis pum-pum, no matter how much joke you tell."

"But kiss me neck!" Aloysius exclaimed, with surprise.

The old woman, aware that the jokes had stopped and lunatic talking begun, shot him a worried glance.

"Wha' happen?" she asked.

"You pum-pum talking rudeness to me!"

A look of alarm appeared on her face.

"What you talking about?"

"You pum-pum! You don't hear what it just say?"

"Me is a Christian pum-pum. No Madman goin' ride me behind no bush," the pum-pum snapped.

"Pum-pum must be seen and not heard!" Aloysius said angrily.

"Lord God Almighty!" the old woman shrieked. "A fit o'madness catch him. Him goin' chop off me head!"

"Help! Police! Madman want ride me!" the pum-pum bawled.

"Hush you mouth!" Aloysius hissed, pointing a chastising finger at the impertinent pum-pum.

The old woman wrestled her basket away from him and flew down the road, scattering fruit after her.

"Madman chasing me! Help!" she bleated as she ran.

"Murder! Hood!" her pum-pum cried.

"Stop, you rass you!" Aloysius shouted. "Come back! Me not going trouble you!"

But the old woman was already over the hill and running pell-mell towards the village square.

Aloysius sat down on an embankment of the roadway and shook his head.

"Why every rass thing on dis island, even pum-pum, must try and chat wid me, eh?" he wondered aloud.

"Why, indeed?" echoed a nearby bush.

"Is because you is de only sensible man in dese parts, who have ears dat listen," said a green lizard sunning itself on a rock.

"Backfoot and crosses," Aloysius moaned, holding his head.

"De times hard on every man," said the bush sorrowfully.

His brain confused, Aloysius sighed.

The searing sun beat down on his head like a blast of hot air out of a parson's mouth.

He was sitting so against the embankment when he suddenly remembered what he was to do today, and he remembered too why he had forgotten it: because it was a thing he did not much like to do, but a thing he had promised another man he would do. It was a thing to do with the sea, and Aloysius was one man who was not fond of the sea.

If it could be said that there are two classes of men, the ones who love the land and those who love the sea, then Aloysius emphatically belonged to the first class. All his life he had been a lover of land, a hater of the sea. The land put food in his belly and it gave him a place to sleep and in the morning when he woke up and stared around him, the land was always there, waiting for him like a faithful nurse. The land sat under your feet like an old bone and did not quiver or shake except during an earthquake. And though the trees would rustle and the grass might whisper in a breeze, the land itself was a tongue-less, voice-less thing. It was a thing of great beauty, and even a hungry man like Aloysius occasionally had an eye for the kingly sweep of a mountain or the lilting curve of a grassland. He could reach out and touch the land, and feel its warmth during the night, and imagine that under his touch lay the flesh of a beautiful woman.

One night, one dark and lonely night when Aloysius was sleeping under a tree, when the loneliness gnawed at his heart so that he wanted to whimper like a child, when his hood stood up stiff and disciplined like a soldier parading before the Governor General. He had even made love to the land. He had dug a hole in the loose dirt with his finger and he heaped the dirt around the hole so that it was conical and soft like a small anthill. And then in the darkness, with the incessant chatter of bushes all around him, he had driven his hood into the land and worked it slowly, pretending that the land was a woman. And to tell the truth, it felt just like an old woman's pum-pum. It was grainy and hard and had no juice whatsoever, but the hunger for pum-pum was upon him with such a fever that he had only to thrust three times into the ground and the thing was done with a loud groan.

But even then it was not over. Even though all this took place in the dark of night in an open bushland with nothing but darkness and emptiness and stars as witnesses, even so it was bound to draw censure, comment, criticism. For everything that Aloysius did, no matter what time of night or day, was bound to draw comment. That was the cross of his madness. A parson could masturbate in the bedroom of his manse three times in one night and next morning go out and preach damnation and warts to onanistic schoolboys and no one would be any the wiser. A government minister could grind the daylights out of his young maid from the country all night long and next morning still deliver a bombastic speech against moral turpitude to Parliament. But let a homeless madman grind even the ground and God knew that every bush in the vicinity, every tree, every weed, ant, cockroach, mouse, or passing mongoose that had seen him relieve himself so would raise its tongue against him.

This time it was a dirty bush that shouted out loud, "Kiss me Granny, him fuck de ground!"

And when Aloysius, who had nearly jumped out of his skin with fright, hissed, "shhhhhh!" and put his finger frantically over his lips, the bush redoubled its cry like one bellowing for a constable, "Him fuck de ground! Madman just fuck de ground! Now ground goin' hatch mad pickney!"

And all over the grassland the cry was taken up and repeated:

"What dat? Him fuck de ground?"

"Who fuck de ground?"

"Aloysius fucking de ground! Pass de word!"

"Rass! De ground! Even de virgin ground no safe from hood!"

"De ground! De innocent ground that don't trouble nobody, and now man come fuck it! But kiss me neck, Lawd God Almighty, what is dis now?"

"Ground fucker!"

And there was such an outcry you would have thought a local magistrate had caught his woman in the bush giving pum-pum to a foreigner. Finally, Aloysius had grabbed his machete and chopped down the bush that had raised the alarm and when the first chop of the machete rang through the darkness the silence of night and death fell on the bushland.

Yet he had had to move from that section of the bushland and could never sleep there again because of malicious whispers that trailed after him. Once a bush had a nasty name to call you, once it knew something about your private life, it never let you forget. That was the way of bushes – malicious and prosecutorial like an old widow woman whose longing for hood turns her into a backbiter.

But even with all this tribulation, the sea was still a greater trouble. The sea was an eye that sometimes stared at you with a nasty blue, and sometimes looked green, and sometimes shone white and ugly like the glare of an albino. It licked ceaselessly at everything – bone or rock or reef or dead body. It lapped your foot like a cunning dog; it fawned and pretended to be your friend. It whispered and purred and sang like a mother and waited. For always the sea was waiting. Watching. Aloysius did not trust the sea. He did not like fish. He did not like anything that had to do with the sea – fishing or diving or even swimming. And though he sometimes went swimming in the sea, he never ventured out too far, never to such a distance that the blue pupil of the great eye yawned fathomless and dark and underneath him.

Yet today he was to do a thing in the sea, and that is why his mind had made him forget it. He was to go with a man who owned a canoe. They intended to row up alongside the tourist ship that would be in the harbour today and sing for the passengers and beg them to throw coins into the water. One of the men in the canoe would then dive into the sea after the coins.

Which man? Not the one who owned the canoe, certainly. This man was the white man – the Backra, the Busha, the

Boss – whatever name you gave him, he was not the one who threw his body into the sea and went after the coins. It was the other one who did the diving – for half the money.

And that is what Aloysius had promised an Indian fisherman he would do today.

"Backfoot and crosses," he moaned.

His belly began to bawl with hunger. Sweetsops and naseberries will fill a schoolchild's belly for breakfast, but the belly of a grown man wants meat or grain.

So Aloysius sat on the wall and shuddered at what lay ahead of him today. His belly wanted food and his hood wanted pum-pum and his mind wanted not to think about the sea.

"So what you goin' do, den?" asked the bush, in the fault-finding voice of an arithmetic teacher.

"Mind you own rass business," the lunatic replied, bowing his head while he studied his miseries.

Chapter Six

What Aloysius did was go to Ocho Rios, as he had promised, and he dove deep into the dark blue eye of the ocean beside the great white ship that seemed cemented to the water, and he retrieved the coins that came tumbling out of the sky.

He dove for three, four hours. At first the passengers crowded the railings of the towering decks of the ship, and the silver coins came spinning out of the sky as he imagined snow must look – he had seen snow only in the moving pictures. He would throw himself headlong into the sea and scan for the flash of silver as the coin wobbled towards the bottom, and sometimes he would be lucky and grab the money before it was swallowed by the darkness of the ocean. But sometimes he would be too slow and the coin would drift into the darkness and he would glimpse, as he lunged for it, the shrouded ugliness of the ocean liner's great underbelly hulking in the depths, and the sight would fill his heart with terror. Sometimes he would even brush against the dark, swollen belly of the great ship and feel its slimy bottom caressing his skin. Then he would hurry to the surface and clamber quickly aboard the canoe, panting for breath, and the cries of the passengers and shouts of the other divers would ring in his ear like the distant sounds of the world awakening a sleeper from a fearful dream.

The owner of the canoe scowled whenever Aloysius broke the surface empty-handed. He was an East Indian with a crooked scar down the fleshy part of his nose and it was whispered that in his pocket was a sharp knife that he aimed at the throat whenever he became enraged.

"Damn negar man breathe too damn much," he scowled at Aloysius. "You losing all de money because o' you damn breathing."

Aloysius did the diving for the few hours that the tourists were amused throwing coins over the side of the great ship and seeing the black men dive for them, but finally it came to be early afternoon when the sun scalded the sea and heat waves shimmered off the zinc roofs of the town, and with the heat the tourists disappeared from the railing and the divers rowed back to shore.

On the beach the East Indian counted out the coins, fondling them between his calloused fingers, putting each one up to his nose and sniffing it suspiciously. And when the dividing was done and each man had his share, Aloysius hurried to a nearby shop to buy lunch.

He bought a tin of bully beef and two bullahs and he paid for the food with the coins, sliding them on the dirty counter to the woman on the other side who eyed him warily as she counted out the change, then he wandered through the crowded square and down to the beach where he could find a place to eat his lunch.

The bully beef was wonderful for his belly. It had fat in it and his belly loved fat more than anything else it could eat. He swallowed the meat so fast that he hardly chewed it, and when it got to his belly, his belly was so glad for the fat that it gave off a muffled noise like a respectable widow passing wind in a church. The bullah was dry and had a slight taste of saltfish, but still it felt good to have the weight of the doughy gingerbread in his belly, and when he had finished eating lunch he felt as full as a rich man after dinner.

He felt so full that he wanted to sleep. But he could not sleep in the hot sun, nor could he sleep on the beach. Soon now the schoolchildren would be out of school and would wander down to the beach to do mischief. If they saw a madman sleeping under a tree, they would stone him with their slingshots or sneak up on him and drop a green lizard on his slumbering belly. Both these things the older schoolboys had already done to Aloysius. It was a great horror to be awakened by the icy pods of a lizard scrambling over the hairs on one's chest.

He started up the road that led away from the town, looking for a place to sleep. It was only when sleep caught him during the day that he wished he had a house. At night the darkness was a house enough for every man. But during the daytime hours when the sun was hot and the breeze did not blow, when the John Crow circled high in the still air over the bony land, any man would wish that he had a house to go to and a bed to sleep on.

He trudged down the road until he came to a trail that wound through the thicket on the hillside. He took the footpath and shouldered his way into the bush, following the bed of a small stream that trickled down the hill, cutting a groove in the soft, brown earth. Finally, he arrived at a clearing and curled up against the trunk of a towering mango tree whose blossoms scented the woods with a soft perfume.

Here he fell asleep.

Here, too, he met the white woman.

She took photographs of his erect hood.

For when a man has not had a woman for months, when he has had only the ground to grind, the hood of such a man will rise in his sleep. It doesn't much matter who controls Parliament, what the Queen Mother says, or how much the parsons might rave against it, when a hood has had no pum-pum for two years it will rise like the Union Jack in the glory days of the Fallen Empire. It will ascend into the air like a bishop into a pulpit, a muffin in an oven.

So as Aloysius slept his hood rose up and flew over the tattered fly of his pants, stiff and stylized like the American flag on the moon.

And the white woman took photographs of it.

She had been sitting behind a bush with her camera, trying to take pictures of doctor birds hovering around the blossoms of the mango tree. Aloysius had not seen her when he first tramped into the clearing, and she had remained perfectly still and watched while he settled on the ground and fell asleep.

Then she saw his hood rise and aimed her camera.

She took a distant shot. She came closer and photographed a dorsal view of the risen hood. She moved to the right and got a lateral shot. Then to the left and got another lateral shot. If only the idiot would sleep for a day or two she thought, she could get more film, take enough shots to make a dirty book.

Her heart was beating fast as she quietly moved around the clearing, taking care to snap no twig, step on no dry leaf, startle no bird. She shot hood in foreground with tree in background, hood in background with bush in foreground; then, adjusting the focus of her camera, she shot hood and bush together, then hood with tree, hood without tree, then hood in sharp focus against a background of the green blur of foliage. Front view, side view, back view, overview: she stalked around the hood like a predator, the camera clicking.

She was exultant as she worked. Others had come to Jamaica before her; others would come after her. But the others returned to Germany, where she had come from, with pictures of a waterfall, an ocean view, a terraced green mountain. She would take back pictures of an aboriginal hood in a clearing beside a brook. Hood shot from every angle. Candid, unrehearsed shots.

She heard a faint buzz of wings, looked up and saw a doctor bird hovering before the blossom of the mango tree. Her heart leaped with joy. She stooped down and tried to get a shot of hood in foreground and bird in background. But the bird flew too high, the hood too low. So she lay down and slithered on her belly up to the hood, the camera mounted over her eye, trying to get hood and bird together.

As if it suspected that it was being used in pornography, the bird prudishly flitted to another blossom.

The woman was creeping towards Aloysius, her camera aimed at his stiff hood, trying to get a shot of hood foreground, bird background, wondering whether she should climb the tree and try for bird foreground, hood background, and muttering curses under her breath because the stupid bird kept restlessly moving without any regard for art, when Aloysius woke up.

He woke up, blinked groggily, and saw a white woman with a metal eye creeping on the ground towards him.

He screamed with terror and scurried behind a bush.

Another woman would have dropped her camera and fled the clearing. But this one knew kung-fu, karate, judo. When Aloysius first screamed, she thought he meant to attack her. Dropping the camera, she assumed the menacing crouch of a Sumo wrestler and stalked boldly towards the bush.

Aloysius threw himself on the ground and hid his face in his hands.

"Blood claat!" he shrieked. "White Witch of Rose Hall! Corpie! Help!"

Even the bush he cowered behind became frightened.

"Shit!" the bush hissed. "No hide behind me, man! You goin' make her chop me up."

She saw that he was frightened, stood up, and opened her palms in a gesture of peace. Aloysius got off the ground cautiously and peeped up at her.

"Where you eye?" he whimpered.

"Eye? Vhat eye?"

"You metal eye. Where it go?"

The woman looked puzzled, then she laughed.

She picked up the camera and showed it to him.

"This is vhat you saw," she said, chuckling.

"You don't have metal eye?"

"Here is my real eye," she said, prying her right eyelids wide open and showing the dark blue of the Aryan eye.

"Rass," he said to himself, standing up and dusting himself off.

"I frighten you. I am very sorry."

"Cho, man!" Aloysius scowled. "Me look up and all me see is one metal eye creeping up 'pon me. What me to think? Me think you was a big insect. Me say, rass, where dem get bug so big in Jamaica? Me say, blood! De bug goin' eat me like bird eat worm. Must frighten me, man! Cho!"

"I understand," she said. "I vas behind that bush, trying to take pictures of doctor birds. You fell asleep before I could say anything."

"So why you creeping 'pon ground, ma'am?"

"I take photographs of that."

Aloysius stared at her as she pointed to the open flap of his pants. He turned quickly and tucked in his hood.

"Me hood? You take picture o' me hood while me sleep?"

"Ja," she chuckled. "I think maybe I send my photographs to the Tourist Board to use in their posters."

"But see here, Jesus Lawd Almighty!" Aloysius bellowed.

"What a out of order woman!" the bush behind him hissed.

"Mind your own business," Aloysius snapped at the bush.

"Imagine," another bush took up the cry, "de man come lie down to rest him head cause de daytime sun hot and him tired, and while him sleep, dis rude white woman come take picture o' him hood! You ever hear anything go so in all you born days? What is dis, Oh Lawd, that Jamaica come to? See how de damn slack foreign woman dem go on nowadays?"

"Dunn's River Falls not good enough for dem anymore. Now dem want shoot picture o' hood too," chorused another.

"What happen to white sand beach, Blue Mountain, boy on donkey, conch shell, and tropical sunset? Now is only hood dem want photograph. Dem soon goin' stop parson in de street and say 'Drop you pants so me can photograph Jamaica parson hood'. You see what de rass world come to?"

The bushes were babbling so indignantly and so thickly that Aloysius screamed at them. "Hush up you rass mouth! Is me hood she photograph, no yours. Make me talk to de woman meself!"

"Who do you talk to?" the woman asked suspiciously.

"De bush dem, ma'am. Dem say you out of order, come photograph me hood when me sleeping. Me no trouble you, ma'am! Me sleeping here minding me own business, you is out o' order to come photograph me hood, ma'am! You come to me country. Is me country dis! You come and visit me country, and you is very welcome like de Prime Minister say 'pon de radio. But you is out of order to come take picture o' me hood, ma'am! Out of order!"

"You talk to bushes?"

"Bush talk to me. Me no talk to bush. Me no business wid no bush!"

"You're a madman!" she squealed.

His eyes blazing, Aloysius could not help but rage at her foolish reasoning.

"Me sleeping in de bush, me not troubling anybody. You creeping 'pon de ground taking picture o' me hood. Which one is de madder one?"

"A lunatic!" The woman breathed excitedly. "This is vonderful."

"Listen to me, ma'am," Aloysius grated, losing his temper. "Me is a peaceful man. Me no trouble nobody. De Prime Minister say no call white man no name in de street, so me no call you no name. Me no call you mad. Me no go to you country and take snapshot o' you hood ..., sorry, I mean, you pum-pum. But you is out o' order ..."

"You don't frighten me," she said calmly. "I show you."

She took a deep breath, and the sound of the breath being drawn was a horrible one, like the hissing a child might hear under its bed on a dark night. And when she had sucked in the breath, she crouched low and approached the mango tree, moving in sinister, jerky steps.

She stood panting beside the tree for a moment, breathing heavily like a bitch in heat on a hot day. But then a fearful and guttural shriek erupted out of her belly. Her body exploding in a violent spasm her hand flashed through the air and struck a limb of the tree, splintering it off at the trunk.

The tree uttered a piercing scream.

"Blood!" the tree howled. "She chop off me limb! Blood!"

"Shit house mouse!" a bush whispered.

"Blood Town!" muttered Aloysius.

"So easy I kill a man," she whispered, uncoiling slowly.

"Me no trouble dis woman, sah!" the tree bawled. "Is dis damn madman loose outta de asylum come trouble her. So what she do? She chop off me hand! Jesus God Almighty, she chop off me hand!"

"Hush up!" Aloysius grated, his heart beating with fear. "Is only one little limb. You have plenty more!"

"Now who you talk to?" the woman scowled.

"De tree, ma'am," Aloysius mumbled. "Him bawling dat you chop off him hand."

The woman threw back her head and bellowed a maniacal, frenzied laugh – laughter such as Aloysius had never heard outside of the madhouse.

"This is vonderful!" she exulted. "Look vhat I do today. I photograph a doctor bird. I take pictures of – vat you Jamaicans call it – a hood. And I meet my first madman. I feel like my holiday just begins now in Jamaica."

"Bumbo," the bush whispered. "New kind of woman, dis."

Chapter Seven

In the clearing beside the stream that guttered a slow wound in the brown earth, Aloysius stood with the white woman. The tree was shrieking bad words because the woman had cut off its limb. The bushes were hissing about the wickedness of foreigners. Stooping, the woman was writing in her notebook as Aloysius watched from a respectful distance.

She was writing down in her book that at this very moment she had met a madman on her holiday to Jamaica. Before she started to write, she had asked Aloysius the time of day so she could record the exact moment in her book. Aloysius said he had no watch and did not know what time it was, so she burrowed into a big bag, fished out a watch and recorded the time in her book.

The tree was a profane tree. Even as the white woman wrote down words in her book and Aloysius looked around and debated whether to run, the tree cursed its fate in a loud voice. It cried "Rass" and "Bumbo" and "Blood" – all filthy words – and bawled out monstrous oaths in such a raucous trumpeting voice that Aloysius finally said, "Listen me, tree, you can't cuss so, you know. God might hear you."

The tree bellowed in reply, "No talk no shit in me ear, you rass! Is you make dis woman chop off me limb! Is you cause dis whole thing to happen!"

The woman looked up from her writing, squinted at Aloysius and asked if he was still talking to the tree. Aloysius nodded and said that the tree was bawling because she had chopped off its limb.

"Rass hole!" the tree yelped. "No tell dis rass woman nothing 'bout me, you hear me, sah? No tell de rass woman what me say!"

And so the woman wrote, the tree cursed loudly, and Aloysius stood beside the stream trying to decide whether to run.

"No rest for de wicked," a nearby bush moaned like an old woman at a funeral.

It was a tense moment for Aloysius. He did not know what to do. He wanted to say something harmless and polite such as, "Good day, then," and quickly leave. But this was no ordinary woman. She was strong and violent: she might grab a stone and bludgeon him to death. She might bite off his toes. She might wrestle him to the ground and pass wind repeatedly in his face until he was gassed unconscious. God only knew if she was even a real woman or something worse.

Yet he calmed himself by remembering that more than once he had had to cope with strong women, violent women. Jamaican country women were strong from a hard life of labouring beside their men in the fields, violent from a love of hood and rum. The parsons held evangelical revivals on the island constantly but Jamaican country women still loved hood and rum. So they were made by the Almighty. When they were drunk they either wanted to beat a man or give him pum-pum until his back was broken. It made no difference that these women carried a soft wet spot between their legs. Their bodies were still hung with stringy sinews and sharp bones. They broke heads and smashed bones and bit off noses and ears in fights just like the men. Some of them were strong enough to squeeze a hood so tight during lovemaking as to make any man bawl for mercy.

What was different about this woman, other than her violent strength and fearlessness, was her white skin. Aloysius was not at all used to such a white woman. All the white women he had seen in the streets had puffy bellies that jiggled when they walked, mounds of flesh that bounced off their arms and chests. The bodies of the old ones looked spongy, watery; the young ones were ungainly, bony – like new-born calves.

But this white woman was short and thick as a tree stump. Her arms were big and coiled with muscles, her eyes the dark and menacing blue of the deep sea. Powerful, stubby legs and fleshy knees swelled through the fraying cuffs of her shorts. She looked hard and solid as though God meant her to be a bronze statue on a public park.

Done with her writing, the woman stood up, yawned, and put away her book in a bag. Then she stretched so hard that Aloysius heard a bone crack.

"My name is Inga Schmidt," she said, holding out her hand.

Aloysius shook it. He had not shaken a hand in at least twenty years. He had not held a hand affectionately since he was a young boy. Even the old woman who had given him the pum-pum years ago had not held his hand. What had happened between them had involved only his hood stabbing blindly at her dry pum-pum in the shadow of a bush. The hand had had nothing at all to do with it.

"Vhat is your name?" she asked.

Aloysius began. He did not want to tell her his entire name, but he could not help himself.

"Aloysius Gossamer Longshoreman Technocracy Predominate Involuted Enraptured Parliamentarian Patriarch Verdure Emulative Perihelion Dichotomy Chase Iron-Curtain Linkage Colonialistic Dilapidate …"

"Vait!" she said, holding up a finger. "Just a moment."

Aloysius scowled at the interruption, but then he remembered what her hand had done to the tree.

"How many names have you?" she asked.

"A thousand names!" he said boastfully. "Me have a thousand names."

She took out the book.

"Start from the beginning again," she said, "I vill write them all down."

"Bumbo Claat," whispered the bush. "Watch dis now."

They sat down under the tree, which was still whimpering over its injury.

Aloysius began.

"Aloysius Gossamer Longshoreman Technocracy Predominate Involuted Enraptured …"

"Don't go so fast," she snapped. "My English is not so good."

It went this way. He would say one of his names, and she would be unable to spell it.

"How do you spell Verdure?" she asked.

"Me can't spell, ma'am!" he scowled.

"So how can you have a name you can't spell?"

"Is me name, ma'am! Me can't spell it, but is me name!"

"Damn it! I can't spell it neither. I vant to write this down in my book. But my English is not good! Vhat are ve to do?"

"Bumbo! Make me tell me name, ma'am! Me brain can't take all de pressure o' interruption!"

"I cannot spell Verdure!" Her blue eyes blazed a dangerous fire. "I cannot write down vhat I cannot spell! I know six languages, but I cannot spell any of them! This is your language, vhy can't you spell your own name?"

Aloysius screamed his anguish, his humiliation, his sorrow.

"Because me can't read!"

She glared at him stonily, unsympathetically, the book poised in one hand, the pencil in another. Then she began to curse rapidly, her eyes still piercingly fixed to his face, each obscenity popping in the quiet clearing like the distant sound of a child being slapped.

"Shit shit shit shit piss piss piss piss fuck fuck fuck fuck cock cock cock cock pussy pussy pussy pussy modderfucker modderfucker modderfucker. There! Now I feel a little better."

Aloysius stared at her with bewilderment.

"Vell," she sighed, putting away her book, shouldering her knapsack. "It is no use. I can't write down your names if ve both cannot spell. So, come. Ve go now. My name is Inga. You can tell me your names when ve valk. Come on. I vant to hear them all."

They started down the path that led to the roadway.

Aloysius spoke his names, slowly, carefully, for the benefit of the foreigner.

"Impracticable Loquacious Predilection Abomination Vichyssoise Pyrrhic Mountebank ..."

"You know vhat I need is a guide," she said. "Vould you like to be my guide? I have money. I pay you to show me Jamaica."

"Unconscionable Altercation Lookalike Partition Bosky Pigeon-toed Dentition ..." Aloysius rattled on obdurately, determined not to answer until he had recited all his names.

"De blind leading de blind," a bush moaned.

"Bitch and brute! Don't come back to dis place!" the tree screamed after them as the surrounding undergrowth brushing the narrow footpath swallowed them up.

In the old days the first tourists who came to Jamaica were English. They had pale faces, chilly manners, and distracted eyes. They were a belchless, fartless, scented people and in their presence the Jamaicans who met them and served them and who of necessity under the strictures of the Almighty's plan were bound to occasionally belch and fart and stink, felt small and worthless like unloved children. These first English tourists perpetually said "Pardon" even when they had done nothing to be pardoned for and caused generations of Jamaicans to wince as though that innocuous word was an order for a flogging.

In the later days after the Empire had fallen the tourists were Americans: men with enormous bellies bulging through distended cotton shirts painted with shrill pictures of yellow sunsets, green parrots, and pink fish; women with blood-red lips and enamelled fingernails whose bodies dripped with jewellery like fruit from a bountiful tree. The English had sniffed silently at the land like strange dogs in a strange place and gathered on verandas in the evenings to the clinking of ice and the fluorescent glow of their own whiteness; but the Americans played on the land – romping in the streets during the daytime hours like noisy schoolchildren, fornicating during the nights on dark beaches, their white rumps pumping feverishly under the tropical skies.

In these newest of days most of the tourists were Americans, and a few were English, but many were Germans – people of a growling tongue and the dogmatic mien of a parson sermonizing about hellfire to a Sunday School. Blonde, blue-eyed, these new tourists resembled the Americans in many ways, except that their big bellies were not wrapped in gaudy cotton shirts and they did not smile or laugh as easily as the Americans.

When these Germans first stepped off the airplanes the sun licked greedily at their pale skins like a hungry dog licking meat off an old bone.

Aloysius and the white woman came down the hillside and walked towards Ocho Rios.

The sun was hot and no breeze blew. To their left, the sea lapped against the shore and the dark blue stretched out to the clothesline on the horizon where a few cumulus clouds limply hung. On their right the land reared up thick and luxuriant against the foothills. Ahead of them the rocky bay of Ocho Rios yawned open and chewed on the gristle of the wreathing sea.

"Vhat a lovely island this is," she exclaimed. "I think I never see a place so lovely."

"Life hard here, ma'am," Aloysius said. "De ground hard. Bush talk too much. Everywhere you go you see cow and goat."

"Vhat do bushes say to you?"

"Dey like to chat odder people business. Dey love gossip, ma'am."

In his mind, he was hearing the bush shrieking, "Kiss me Granny, him fuck de ground."

"Dey don't mind deir own business," he glowered, his mind still on the humiliation he had suffered from bushes.

"Sounds like my father," she said darkly.

A dog ambled past, its teats so swollen and pendulous that they scraped the asphalt of the roadway.

"What madman doing wid white woman?" the dog muttered.

Aloysius turned and glared at it.

Chapter Eight

Arithmetic. That was the worry between them. Bad arithmetic. You do not learn arithmetic in the lunatic asylum. You do not learn it from sleeping in the bush or talking to trees. You learn arithmetic the way children have always learned it – out of the mouth of a terrifying teacher while you sit on a hard bench and dream of climbing trees and floating down rivers. Arithmetic was a discipline. It required brain power and concentration. You had to concentrate on the numbers and learn the laws that governed them. And when you knew arithmetic well, it could be your pastime. You could spend a day counting the clouds floating overhead or calculating the weight of fish. You could sit in a forest and count trees or number the leaves on a fern.

The woman sat on a mountain top smoking ganja and doing these very things as Aloysius watched. First she counted all the trees she could see from where she sat, and then she numbered their leaves and wrote the figure down in her book. She said afterwards that she desired a problem to do with gravity and she worried her brain about it then said she could not recall the formula. And after she had smoked the second weed, she wished out loud that they had kidnapped a physicist so she could torment him with an enigma of arithmetic.

She smoked ganja more than Aloysius had ever seen any other woman smoke it. It was the Sinsemilla weed that she smoked – the strong one that made the mind of a grown man fly like a bee – and after she had smoked the second weed on the hillside, then she started to calculate the weight of fish.

If one fish had a girth of so many inches, she wondered out loud, and its flesh weighed so many ounces to a cubic inch, how much would a fish of a certain length weigh? Aloysius had not smoked the weed except for one long drag, which was just as well because the problem to do with fish puzzled his mind and made him feel dizzy. He did not think it was the right thing to do on an afternoon – to sit under a tree on a hillside, smoke weed, and calculate the weight of invisible fish.

But then the whole afternoon in the company of this white woman had been a bizarre time.

They had walked to Ocho Rios, and the eyes of the townspeople had trailed after them like mosquitoes. Bushes whispered as they strolled past. Everyone turned and looked and wondered what a white tourist woman was doing in the company of a ragged lunatic.

Because of the attention he was getting, Aloysius became puffed up and boastful. He told jokes and pretended that he was a lawyer with a house in the country. But no matter that the woman was a foreigner and unused to the ways of Jamaica, it was obvious that she saw through his lies. His clothes were still ragged and tattered and he still had the dishevelled look of one who lived outdoors like a bird at the mercy of God – one on whose bare head everything in the sky must eventually fall: dew, rain, darkness, and the noiseless breath of the sun.

During one of his lies, the woman turned her blue eyes on him and said, "I think you full of shit," which shamed him and made him shut up.

So from then on – and by that time they were through the square of Ocho Rios, past the curious eyes that flicked at them from shop awnings, roadside stands, donkey carts, and burglar-barred windows; past the mutterings that ominously rose in their wake; and walking towards the scenic road that is known as Fern Gully and is a favourite of tourists exploring in rented automobiles – from then he told her only the truth about himself, or tried to tell the truth even if he did not really know it.

But some things he could not tell her even when she asked. He could not tell her when he had first gone mad because he had never gone mad. He could say when the world had first proclaimed him mad and why: it was because he had gotten into a heated roadside argument with a Trinidadian donkey in the Clarendon village of Parnassus. He could tell her what it felt like to be draped up by a constable, carted off in the belly of the Black Maria Land Rover used by the police to transport unruly prisoners, and driven to a madhouse in Kingston, while the donkey, who had started the argument, incurred no punishment. This was the unjust state of affairs in Jamaica as any poor man could testify to. Let a donkey hold a conversation with a man and the man was not supposed to reply, no matter how serious the provocation, no matter that the donkey propounded preposterous ideas that any sensible man would wish to refute – so long as the man sat still and pretended not to hear the donkey insulting him, he was allowed to roam the streets in freedom. But let the man lose his temper at the rubbish the beast was hurling at him, let him raise his voice to correct falsehood and see what happened to him. He was sent to the madhouse, where he was forced to eat chicken backs and wings and hold conversations with brown men in white coats. But let him ask one of these brown men, let him say – so you say I am mad because I hold a chat with a donkey, but why isn't the donkey also judged mad for holding a chat with a man? – and the paradox of that point escaped the brains of the brown-skin men. Say that too insistently, too often, and they locked you in a room whose walls were padded with rubber and they forced you to eat chicken behinds for dinner – the part of the chicken that is pointed like a spear and in the countryside is called the "Bishop's nose" – the worst part of the chicken to give a man who is accused of chatting too much, since it is said to profoundly affect the tongue of the one who eats it, making him talk incessantly. Even today, even after he had been out of the asylum now for some ten months by his latest calculation, he still could not help himself with chatting because of all the chicken behind the brown-skin doctors had made him eat.

They walked and he talked and the woman was grave and foolish and impertinent, and sometimes she laughed while he ranted on about the injustice he had suffered at the hands of the Jamaican government, and sometimes she made him stop so she could take notes and write down his words in her book.

It was this harmless gesture that had made him so sentimental that he could not control himself – this sight of the white woman writing down his words in her book that made him start to blubber like a child, that forced him to lean against one of those cut-stone mortarless walls that were strung across the Jamaican countryside by anonymous slave hands many years ago, and catch his breath. And when he could not catch his breath, the tears came and he wept along the side of the road in full sight of this woman while she wrote down in her book that the first madman she had met on her holiday to Jamaica was now weeping; wept because in all his life, no man, no woman, no child, no bush, dog, donkey, mule, no one before had ever written down any of his words in a book.

"Hot in the sun," the woman had grunted as he wept.

"Maybe ve find some shade vhen you're through."

But she asked no questions about why he wept.

So it was a bizarre afternoon in the company of the stout white woman who wrote words in her book and carried a big bag on her back.

After they had walked up through the Fern Gully road, drawing prying stares from the people in shops they passed, after she had asked him questions about his madness and after he had wept, she asked if he would show her the real Jamaica as if the ground under their feet were imaginary and the sky over their heads a dream.

He took her into the bush. They left the asphalt road and followed a footpath that pierced through a thickly wooded grove, ascending into the back country where small cultivators lived and cows and goats grazed. Everywhere they looked the land was green and shining, for the afternoon rains had already fallen, and the smell of the moist earth rose up around them like the odour from a freshly bathed woman.

Then the foreigner went to work on the land with her camera. She pointed it everywhere, and it made a small noise like the sound of biting. It bit at bushes and valleys, at mountains and at the sweeps and folds of the green earth. It bit at flowers and at birds, and sometimes it even nibbled at the clouds and the sky.

Some of the bushes loved to be photographed and some did not love it so well. Some screamed at the woman when the camera snapped at them, and others giggled and complained that they were ticklish. Aloysius held himself aloof from the clamour, would answer no impertinent questions put to him by the bushes, and walked meekly in the tracks of the foreign woman while she stooped and bent and climbed and lay on the ground to take pictures. The camera gnawed restlessly at the land all afternoon.

But eventually they had come to the mountaintop and to the time when the woman, her eyes red from smoking too much ganja, began calculating the weight of invisible fish. They had climbed into the deep bushland, where – except for the small sounds of birds – the land was green, dignified, calm, and silent like the depths of the ocean. Under a tree they sat, the woman smoking ganja, Aloysius worrying about what he would eat for dinner.

It was here that the woman gave him the pum-pum.

It did not matter that she had hair all over her body or that she had legs as thick as fence posts, she should not have beaten him.

It did not matter that she was a white foreigner who had spent the greatest part of the afternoon smoking the strongest ganja grown in Jamaica, and it did not matter that she was uncouth enough to have crawled on her belly to photograph his hood while he slept. He would still insist to his last breath that she should not have beaten him.

He explained the circumstances to the flame heart tree under whose boughs he had slept for the past two years and the tree was entirely of the same mind. No foreign woman should come to Jamaica and beat a Jamaican citizen.

It is a horrible state of affairs that a man suffers when a woman beats him. It causes wounds greater than any fist or stick can give. Such a thing sticks in a man's mind to the end of his days. Like an injustice, it returns to torment him whenever he is depressed or sad. It is the kind of injury that requires public expression of indignation and outrage for a man to get over, and so Aloysius that very night told the tree about how the woman had beaten him, and the tree was sympathetic and vocal in its disapproval.

"Damn out of order," the tree muttered.

Could he have helped himself? After an abstinence of nearly two years – the last time had been with the dry pum-pum of an old woman who had stolen his supper – after he had been reduced to grinding the ground itself, after he had not seen a pum-pum for all this time, could he be held responsible or at fault over the behaviour of his starving hood?

"Rude!" the flame heart tree agreed truculently. "De woman is rude and out of order!"

For when the woman offered herself to him, wriggled out of her drawers and bared to him the reddest pum-pum he had ever seen in his life, a thing nestled fat and deep between her legs, a thing that struck him very like a certain kind of shy red fish who lives in a dark part of the reef under a ruff of waving seaweed – for so the pum-pum seemed to him as it peeped out at him from between the dark crevice of her legs – his hood had jumped up like a corporal on the parade ground, and his mouth was so dry from the pounding of his heart that he could not talk, could not even clear his throat as she wrestled him down on top of her.

What happened next was the kind of lovemaking that parsons hate because it has nothing to do with love, kissing, fondling, hand, feet, ears and mouth and noses, nor any other part of the body except hood and pum-pum – the parts utterly ungovernable by religion and preaching, the parts that obdurately pay no collection in church, endure no hymn singing, no shrieking to the Holy Ghost by old women at a prayer meeting. It was lovemaking in which the hood and pum-pum whispered to one another in a private tongue like two lawyers outside a courthouse.

Then he was inside the pum-pum, which was in spate with its own juices, and he was sinking into a smooth tunnel that had neither walls, top, bottom, sides, beginning, end; a tunnel that one might imagine must be like the belly of a fat, endless eel. It was so slippery and soft that for one dreadful moment he imagined that he would continue to slide in until only the top of his head protruded from between her legs, and he would drown there, vainly shrieking in the clammy darkness for a rope or a ladder.

And if he had stuck there and not shifted or moved everything might have turned out for the better – if he had done what bird shooters do when they find themselves suddenly sinking down to the hips in a soft pocket of a swamp – if he had merely poised there for a moment or two and not savoured how wonderful it felt to have two hairy legs crushing his ribs in a love grip and how sweet to swim deep between a woman's legs where softness itself bubbles and oozes out of her body … .

"What's past is past," the tree said sensibly.

But instead he shifted slightly because of a tormenting fear of disappearing inside her, and it was suddenly over. He groaned and was done.

The fire flared in her eyes and blazed.

"You brute!" she shrieked.

A fist streaked from her side and clouted him a ringing blow on the ear.

He toppled over on the ground. She clambered on top of him and rained blows down on his body.

"No murder me in me own country!" he bawled, trying to shield his face with his hands. "Have mercy!"

"Woman kill man!" a bush screamed with terror.

But the second time he was a little better. She satisfied her rage and smoked another joint of the weed. He gently touched the bruises on his face and shook off the pain of the beating. Then they tried a second time.

This time she rolled on top of him, which was a position he did not especially favour because once a rude woman had

ridden him so and screamed, "Giddayup!" in his ear as though
he were a donkey she was riding to the market. But the white
woman was not so obnoxious as to do such a thing. She merely
rode him with an intensity, a dark fierceness that made his heart
beat fast and his toes twitch. And though he was a little better
and lasted a little longer, he still could not hold out long
enough for her. When it was obvious that he was done again
before she was ready, she screamed so hard in his face that
drops of her spittle rained down on his chest.

She double a fist and drew it back. He winced and closed his
eyes, expecting the blow.

But instead she rolled off him and lit up another of the
Sinsemilla weeds.

The third time he was useful to her.

The third time he was weary and almost unwilling to do it,
but she stroked his hood and it stood up for her like a dutiful
Boy Scout before the Queen. His belly was bawling for hunger
and the bruises on his face stung from his sweat, yet the third
time he managed to last long enough to please her.

When it happened, her face turned as purple as a sea grape;
she kneaded his shoulders with her fists and jerked backwards
as though a bomb had gone off inside her belly.

"O-Isopropoxyphenyl!" she shrieked, causing a ringing in
his ears.

It was, she said afterwards, the word she always shrieked
whenever a hood gave her pleasure. It was a word from
chemistry, which she had studied at the university. She had first
experimented with saying that word some three years ago and
liked it better than anything else she had cried out before.
Since then, it was the word she always said at that time.

"What dat word mean?" Aloysius asked, so weary that he was
lying on his belly in the dirt, unable to move.

"Cockroach poison," she murmured.

"Cockroach poison?"

"Vhy not! Vhat does it matter vhat I say?"

"It don't matter," he whispered.

He was so weary he could hardly stand. His hood was dead. The foreign pum-pum had killed it. That was the way it always went with hood and pum-pum: hood goes in like a lion but comes out like a lamb.

She spat at a bush.

"I need at least two, three, maybe four lovers," she said. "That's how I am. One man cannot satisfy me. I must have at least two."

"Aloysius   Gossamer   Longshoreman   Technocracy O-Isopropoxyphenyl Predominate Involuted ..." Aloysius murmured.

Now he had a thousand and one names.

"A thousand and one names," marvelled the tree jealously. "And me wid only one name."

"What dat name be?" Aloysius wondered, curling up wearily on the ground.

" 'Tree'. What else? Dat what everybody in Jamaica call tree. Just 'tree'."

Aloysius did not stir.

"You don't know how much me wish me had a hood like you," the tree griped. "Me damn tired o' de blossom and de bee business. Damn foolishness every year – blossom and bee. Pollination and cross-fertilization. Me no care what parson say, me'd give me tap root for one good grind. Even if me could grind one o'dem female dog dat, come weewee 'pon me trunk sometime. Instead, is nothing but pure bee and blossom, year in and year out. Bee and blossom."

Aloysius began to snore.

Chapter Nine

A preaching bush woke up Aloysius. It was a bush that claimed to have taken a correspondence course from an American seminary, that sat in a dirty gully and did nothing but rant and rave all day except during the fiercest heat of the sun when it had to content itself with muttering like an old man. Once or twice before, this same bush had awoken Aloysius from a sound sleep with its preaching until he had threatened to chop it up with his machete the next time. Now the bush was waxing full force as though it were in a church being listened to attentively by fifty toothless old women.

"Oh Babylon," the bush shrieked, "what will become of dis Babylon dat we call Jamaica? Where donkey do nothing but bray and grind all day! Where dog want nothing more dan to mount every passing bitch! Where backra and busha lie in wait to grind de poor maid! Where every woman in dis country must caulk up deir pum-pum from ravaging hood! Where de pickney dem don't do deir lessons at night! What will happen to Babylon in dese wicked times? Woe unto ye, Oh Jamaica! Pum-pum and rum gone to your brain and make you giddy!"

"Hush you bumbo!" Aloysius screamed at the bush.

"Is you dat, Missah Aloysius?" enquired the bush timidly, after a thoughtful silence.

"Yes, Rass. And you wake me up!"

"Sorry, sah. But a fit o' preaching catch me!"

"Hush you rass mouth and make me sleep."

The bush was silent for a few moments.

"Missah Aloysius," the bush muttered, "Jamaica man love pum-pum too much!"

"Me say hush you rass!" Aloysius screamed.

But in the silence that followed, even though the morning was only a smudge of chalky light against the darkness, Aloysius could not go to sleep again. His back hurt him from all the grinding of the night before and his throat was dry and parched because of all the vital fluids the pum-pum had squeezed out of him.

"Pum-pum mash me up," he groaned, squirming under the flame heart tree.

"A wish it would mash me up, too," sighed the tree.

"Serve you right," hissed a bush spitefully. "Negar love to grind too much."

Down the road in a big house on the top of a hill, not far from where Aloysius slept, Busha McIntosh was also waking up.

The Busha was the richest man in the parish. His land splashed over fields, licked at the belly of the mountain, and rolled down to the coastline. It was a luxuriant land, fed by wild streams and springs, rich with fruit trees and guinea grass pastures. It supported goats, cattle, fruit trees, rats, and praedial thieves.

Busha had inherited this land from his father, his father from his father, and so on down through a succession of twelve fathers stretching back to the earliest days of Jamaica. The very title of "Busha" – a slave corruption of "overseer" – spoke of ancestry, wealth, land, striking the local ear with the same galvanic ring that initials such as ITT, IBM, GM have on Americans.

A white man whose complexion had been broiled an ugly red by long hours in the tropical sun, Busha still struck an imposing figure in his fifty-fifth year of life. His wife Sarah was fat and cozy like a well-fed cat and had a clever mind for books, balance sheets, and general business.

This morning Busha and Sarah took breakfast on their veranda. All around them the dawn broke open like an egg oozing a thin white light throughout the world.

Maids worked inside the tiled interior of the house while the Busha and Sarah breakfasted. One maid cooked breakfast. The other spread beds and dusted. A garden boy shined the Busha's boots. In the back yard, another garden boy wiped the dew off the Busha's Land Rover.

Settled comfortably in a puddle of middle-aged contentment, Busha and Sarah had been married now these twenty-five years, had raised five grown children, and were each occupied with satisfying pursuits. Busha farmed and reared cattle; Sarah kept books for foreigners and coached the church choir. He fished and hunted birds; she crocheted and scolded maids. Both were devoted to eleemosynary projects in the village – Busha to curbing drunkenness and idleness among adolescent boys, Sarah to promoting matrimony and eliminating teenage pregnancies.

Busha and Sarah had little to say to each other this morning. When a man and a woman have been married for twenty-five years and times are basically good, they do not prattle like new lovers. The small daily issues in their lives are subjected to long-standing treaties, time-honoured procedures, predictable attitudes. There is no use chit-chatting about praedial larceny or the latest murders in Kingston or the slackness of today's youth – for each knows exactly how the other feels and can predict what the other will say. Unanimity on virtually every moral and parochial issue reigned in Busha's household.

If the times had been bad, Busha and Sarah might have gathered themselves in a corner out of earshot of prying maids and begun the morning with gloomy muttering over their daily worries.

But these were not bad times. A few years before, when the Socialists were raving in Parliament about idle land and threatening to confiscate private property all over the island – those were days for muttering to one's wife; when the Prime Minister so roused the rabble with firebrand orations that urchins and vagrants used to scream "pork" at white people in the streets – those were also times that called for domestic muttering.

But those days were long gone now. Today a man did not have to mutter to his wife just because he happened to be rich and white. Sanity reigned in Parliament. Sugar, salt, flour were back on the shelves. The tourists had returned to Jamaica. In times like these a rich man and his wife could lapse into the unconscious ways of old lovers, could sit and drink coffee with dawn stirring around them and remain benignly speechless towards one another.

Unless there happened to be a bone between them.

For sometimes when a man and a woman have been married many years, a bone will come between them. It will be buried deep below the layers of daily affection, small talk, bi-monthly copulation; it will lie between them on the marriage bed, goad them around the breakfast table, jab them in the church pews.

It was the Busha whom the bone tormented and made sleepless. Even now, as he sat nibbling on fish, his wife of twenty-five years no more than ten feet away, he was gnawing restlessly on his bone like an old dog with a toothache.

The Busha was a man of the soil; his brain was of the earth. He could recite rhymes he had learned in school but he did not understand poetry. He could sing songs but he did not like music. He had pictures hanging on the walls of his spacious house but art and artists were as foreign to him as Tierra Del Fuego.

So Busha was no good at expressing his feelings. He was good at tending to the land, growing the guinea grass, farrowing a sow or whelping a dam. He was good at espying a malingerer, trapping a praedial thief, or butchering a cow. But he was no good at telling what was in his heart. And he was too big, too thick a man to sigh over his troubles. If the Busha could sigh so could an ox.

Indeed, there was something oxlike about Busha's features. His face bulged with fat bones. A puffy nose swelled over his mouth, his cheekbones rose up in a mother-lode of prominent ridges, his chin was rounded and blunt like the end of a club. Busha's face reminded one that God had moulded Adam out of dirt: it resembled a rich and arable mountain land suitable for planting coffee.

The Busha peered over the edges of the *Gleaner* at his wife. He saw a capacious forehead, a severely cropped head of hair, the sharp eyes of a mind used to roaming the warrens of balance sheets and triple-columned ledgers.

"What's the matter?" Sarah asked, meeting the Busha's stare.

"It's a damn shame," the Busha said thoughtfully, "what stray animals are doing to the cemetery."

"Nothing wrong with the cemetery," she said decisively.

"It's just a shame, that's all. I'm going to speak to Shubert about it."

"Mummy and Daddy don't mind," Sarah said.

She bit indifferently into a piece of toast.

Sarah said goodbye to the Busha, pecked him on the cheek, and drove off to Ocho Rios. Busha lapsed briefly in and out of gloom.

Gloom came and went with Busha like a summer sprinkle. If for one minute he did brood about an abstract worry, the very next minute he would be thinking about something definite such as butchering a pig. Shaking off his mood with a tremulous heaving of his large frame, Busha drove his Land Road into the village to see Mr. Shubert.

He found Mr. Shubert sitting behind the grimy counter of his small shop next to the cemetery, poring over the exercise book in which he kept his accounts.

So immersed in his exercise book was Mr. Shubert that he did not immediately look up to see who had thumped so loudly across the floor of the shop, scattering swarms of flies over keg, bin, and barrel. Very likely, the shopkeeper surmised, it was someone who owed him money. The mortal and venial sins of borrowing and credit that had been committed against his shop by nearly everyone in the village were all here in the exercise book. No doubt another borrower now stood before his counter ready to mewl for sugar, milk, salt fish, mackerel on credit.

"Shubert!" the Busha barked. "What are you going to do about those blasted animals in the cemetery?"

"Animals, Busha?" Shubert started, quailing before the voice of the only man in the village, aside from the lunatic Aloysius, whose name was not in the exercise book. "What animals, Busha?"

"Those damn animals there, man," the Busha said irritably. "Look out you window. Look at that blasted cow there in the graveyard."

Shubert looked and saw a brindled cow cropping lazily at a hump in the cemetery sward.

"That's Mother May, my wife's mother, that that damn cow is stomping on."

"Yes, sah?" Shubert said feebly.

"That's right where Mother May is buried. Now cow stomping on her head. Damn disrespectful. Now look what else the damn animal is doing to Mother May!"

Shubert looked.

"Is one thing for a damn animal to stomp on the head of a dead woman, Shubert! But good God, man, now de cow is emptying its bowels and bladder on de poor woman's head! Damn out of order, man!"

"But Busha, is not my cow dat one, sah!"

"But you are the sexton of the church, Shubert! You must keep the damn animals out of the graveyard. Who going to do it if you don't? Dammit to hell, man, every animal in the damn parish use the cemetery as a toilet! Your own mother buried there, Shubert. How'd you like a cow to walk all over her? How'd you like a cow to doo-doo on your Mummy?"

Shubert bristled.

"I don't think I would too like it, Busha."

"And one day, Shubert, you going lie in there too. Then you'll see what it feel like for cow to walk 'pon you and use you head as a damn outhouse when you can't get up and shoo dem away!"

Shubert chuckled.

"Me putting fence 'round me grave, Busha."

"Fence! What good fence do? Don't I fence up Daddy and Mummy? I fence up Granddaddy and Grandmummy. They all fence up in there. Go walk down there and look on Daddy graveslab. You know what colour Daddy graveslab is? Brown and black. You ever see brown and black concrete graveslab in your born days, Shubert? De damn goats jump over my fence just so they can get a chance to empty their bowels on concrete. Jamaican goat don't like shit in grass if him can shit on concrete, you know, Shubert. Dey like to hear splash and plop so dey aim for concrete. All de fence in de world not going keep out de goat dat want to shit on your head."

"Busha, sah," Shubert protested, "dem animals is not my own!"

"Too much damn slackness, man!" Busha scowled. "You are the sexton, it's your responsibility to drive de damn animals out of the graveyard. That's the trouble with Jamaica, you know, Shubert! We just don't care about one another in dis country. Poor Mother May never trouble a soul in her life yet she can't even rest in peace because of the damn cows! Is a disgrace, man! A crying shame!"

Silence followed the Busha's tirade. A few heads peeped into the shop to see who was yelling and popped out just as quickly upon glimpsing the Busha.

"All right, Busha," Shubert said in a defeated tone. "I going look after it."

"I don't want see no more cow in de graveyard, Shubert. You understand me? I don't even want to see puss in dere."

"All right, Busha."

"Good. I gone."

Busha stomped out of the shop. The Land Rover coughed and roared away.

Shubert bellowed for his shop boy.

"Richard! Richard, you backside, come to me!"

From the rear of the shop came a faint shuffling as Richard, a rangy country boy, peeped around a corner.

"Yes, sah?"

"Come ya, Richard! Look out de window! What you see?"

Richard peered diligently out the window.

"Me no se nothing, sah!"

"What happen? You eye blind? What you see?"

"Me only see gravestone, sah, and bush, and tree."

"You don't see cow?"

Richard chuckled good-naturedly like one who had suddenly got the answer to a riddle.

"Yes, sah. Me see cow."

"What de rass cow doing in graveyard, boy? Tell me dat! What de damn hell business cow have in graveyard?"

"Is not my cow, sah!"

"I don't care whose rass cow dat is, don't I put in you charge of de graveyard? Don't I tell you last month you is head man over dat graveyard?"

"But me no put de cow dere, Mr. Shubert!"

"De damn cow walk 'pon me mother grave, doo-doo and wee-wee 'pon me mother head in de ground! Damn out of order, man! Dat's de trouble with you damn country negar, you don't give a damn 'bout nothing but pum-pum and rum!"

"But Missah Shubert ..." Richard bawled.

"Me no want hear no excuse outta you! Damn slackness in dis country! You don't have no tradition, no respect for de dead. You make cow and goat and dog use decent people head for a toilet! Out of order! Damn slackness!"

"But Missah ..."

"RUN DE RASS COW OUTTA DE GRAVEYARD INSTEAD O' ARGUING WID ME!"

Richard muttered, ducked out of the shop, and a moment later was hurtling across the graveyard flinging sticks, stones, and obscenities at the animal.

"Cow, you blood! Get offa de people dem head! Move! Blood! Damn nasty negar cow! Move you blood!"

The animal scurried away from the onslaught of shrieking and stoning.

Inside the shop, Mr. Shubert lapsed into a vengeful scrutiny of his credit book, looking for someone whose account was overdue and needed dunning. A young girl approached the counter timidly.

"No credit today!" Mr. Shubert snapped. "Today is cash day!"

"But Mr. Shubert!" the girl protested.

"Don't argue wid me! I don't want hear no argument!"

"But, sah, me Mummy send me to buy a pound o' sugar, sah. Me have de money."

A snarl on his lips, the shopkeeper glared at the little girl, who carefully laid a clammy coin on the counter.

"Damn pickney in Jamaica don't have no manners," Mr. Shubert scowled.

He weighed the sugar, wrapped it in brown paper, and handed it to the girl.

"Never mind de money," he waved airily. "I'll put it down in me book."

"But Mr. Shubert, sah!"

"I trust you," Mr. Shubert bellowed. "Go 'bout you business wid you money."

The girl pocketed the coin and left the shop. Mr. Shubert settled down behind his counter and neatly entered the amount for the sugar in a column below her mother's name.

By the time he had finished writing and adding the amount to the balance, he was whistling.

"Me drive 'way de cow, sah," Richard whined, panting from all his running. "But dem might come back."

"Don't bother me mind 'bout cow," Mr. Shubert said with the abstract air of the hobbyist contentedly at play, "when you dead you dead, and no dead man or woman know de difference whether rain fall or cow wee-wee on dem head."

*   *   *

The cemetery was Busha's bone.

It ate McIntoshes. It had eaten the first father and the second. It had eaten twelve generations of fathers. It gobbled up McIntoshes like a mongoose eats chickens. Fathers, sons, daughters, wives, husbands, cousins, nephews – generations of McIntoshes had been reduced to ugly lumps in its belly.

The Busha loathed and despised the cemetery with an unutterable passion. He could not drive past it without a shudder. He could not stand even to glimpse it out of the corner of his eye. Yet every Sunday during services in the stone chapel that stood on its grounds, with the merest flicker of a glance out the window, he would see a lump in the sward and know that the cemetery was digesting another McIntosh. It was enough to drive the Busha insane to think that this same plot of scruffy green would one day be chewing his bones.

Not that he was afraid of death. Busha was not numbered among those fretful souls who worried about the afterlife. Parsons of every denomination and stripe had assured Busha that there was indeed a heaven and that was enough to satisfy him. Who should know whether or not there was a heaven? A parson, that's who. Busha did not believe in disputing with experts.

Yet Busha still had a strong craving for some final resting place other than this country graveyard: his heart was set on a grand sarcophagus in a Kingston cemetery. He couldn't help himself. God knew that Busha had few vanities, few foibles. He did not drink; he smoked only an occasional cigar; only once in a very rare while did he take a girlfriend on the side. After living for some fifty-four years among women eager to drop their drawers at the first sight of a man, the Busha had bred only two bush babies. Some of his venal relatives had bred fifteen, sixteen. One wretch of a cousin had bred a score or more.

A sarcophagus was his only weakness. He wanted a sarcophagus like rich Syrian families built for themselves in Kingston; a sarcophagus with pilasters, columns, friezes, a marble angel on the roof blowing a trumpet, the family name scrolled on a pediment above the tomb: a sarcophagus impregnable to cows and goats – that's what Busha wanted. He did not want to be swallowed by the same scruffy cemetery that had devoured twelve generations of his family.

But Sarah would have none of it. Her mother and father lay side by side in the cemetery, and already she had picked out a spot for her and the Busha. It was under a lignum vitae tree on a knoll that was always cooled by an afternoon breeze. Beside Mummy and Daddy. Next door, less than an arm's length away, would be the Busha's father.

"A breezy spot!" the Busha said aloud in a voice ringing with contempt.

He was driving slowly along a winding country road that led towards his slaughterhouse.

He did not want a breezy spot, he wanted a sarcophagus. And he could easily afford the grandest one in all the island – except that Sarah wanted the breezy spot beside Mummy.

"If she put me dere, so help me God I going get up and move!" the Busha vowed, grinding his teeth.

He had made this threat to Sarah during their last argument.

"You want to move, move," she had replied in the imperturbable logic that old wives use to bully old husbands. "But I'm resting beside Mummy and Daddy."

"How can you rest with a cow jumping up and down on your head?" the Busha had scowled.

"Don't be an ass, Hubert!" she had snapped.

And so the breezy spot won out over the sarcophagus; one day the cemetery would eat the Busha.

The Busha was shuddering at this horrible, disgusting thought when he spotted the lunatic Aloysius skipping and dancing on the shoulder of the road. Busha braked his Land Rover to a screeching halt and reversed to accost the madman.

Busha and Aloysius went back a long way. Before his first bout of madness, Aloysius had worked for the Busha, living in a back room in the servants' quarters, taking care of Busha's yard and four dogs. The two of them played together on the village cricket team – Aloysius as a spin bowler whose sly delivery fooled opposing batsmen, Busha as a free-whacking batsman who would either hit sixes all morning or be bowled for a duck on the first ball.

Busha stuck his head out of the window of the car.

"Aloysius, you mad or sane today?"

Aloysius skipped over to the Land Rover.

"Mad, Busha? Me mad, sah? When you ever hear dat me mad, Busha?"

"Don't beat around de bush with me, man. Just give me a straight answer! You mad or sane today?"

"But Busha, me is always sane, sah! When you ever hear dat me mad?"

"All right, you listen to me now, Mr. Aloysius!" Busha glowered. "Me don't want you talking to me cows, you hear me, sah?"

"Talk to cow, Busha? When me ever talk to cow?"

"I don't want no argument from you. I just don't want you talking to me cows in de pasture, you hear! Last time you was living in de bush you talk to me cows day and night and de damn cows stop giving milk. Is you talking to me damn cows in the field that mix dem up. Suddenly cow think him is lawyer or parson and not a cow. I don't want no talking to me damn cow in de bush, you hear me, Mr. Aloysius!"

Aloysius sniggered.

"Busha, which cow tell you me was talking to him, sah?"

"I heard you with me own ears. Telling me cow story about movie in de bush! Damn fool! Which cow ever go to a movie? What you telling me damn cow movie story for? You ruin de best milch cow I have with you damn talking! Dat's what's wrong wid Jamaica today – everybody chat too much. Dey chat their foolishness to every blessed creature, even to cow. Well, I don't want you holding no conversation with me cows, you hear me, Aloysius! Or I going get de constable and lock up you backside for trespassing!"

Busha grinded a gear and roared off down the road.

"De cow tell lie on me, Busha!" Aloysius screeched.

But it was too late. The Land Rover was already far down the road, billowing out a cloud of dust.

Aloysius shrugged and went back to his skipping and dancing. No doubt a cow had told a lie about him. He had just woken up and was still groggy and weak from the pum-pum. Sometimes it took him an hour or two after waking to remember where he was and what he had to do. Sometimes when he woke up he could remember only two or three of his thousand names and had to sit very still and recite like a child trying to remember lines from a poem until the names came back to him. Yet the day ahead seemed to him to hold great promise. He would meet the white woman again today and take her on a tour of the parish.

Busha, meanwhile, roared down the paved road and turned onto a marl track winding into his pasture. He was morosely aware that he had taken out his frustrations about the breezy spot on the lunatic.

When Busha did an unfair thing he immediately expected the world to do an unfair thing back to him. Life was basically simple to Busha: it was like a donkey and its tail. Pull the donkey's tail and you get a kick in the face. The affairs of men and nations were nothing more complicated than that. One time Busha had even shared this analogy with a local parson and tried to get the man to use it in a sermon cautioning the people of St. Ann not to pull the donkey's tail. But the parson was too foreign in his thinking to appreciate the truthful simplicity of Busha's philosophy.

"You think I go to seminary, Busha, to give sermon 'bout donkey and him tail?" the parson asked indignantly. "Is dat I go to university for?"

So of course Busha's message never got to the congregation because it didn't muddle things up enough. Nowadays everything had to be fuzzy to please a parson.

In any event, Busha had taken out his anger on Aloysius – he had pulled the donkey's tail – and now the donkey had the whole day ahead to kick him in the face.

A few minutes later, Busha parked at his makeshift slaughterhouse where an old Ford Escort sitting under a tree told him that the agricultural inspector, a Mr. Nettleton from St. Ann's Bay, was waiting.

"Morning, Mr. Nettleton," the Busha said, shaking hands with the inspector.

"How are you today, Busha?" the inspector greeted him genially.

"Fine, man, fine. Sorry I'm a little late. I had to stop down the road and scold a madman who lives in dese parts."

"Yes, sah?"

"Everytime he goes mad he hold conversation with me cattle. I catch him one day telling me cow about a movie. Imagine that, eh? The poor cow didn't know whether him was coming or going."

"Confusing you cow, eh, Busha?"

"Damn out of order, man! One time he talk so much to one of me cows that she stop giving milk. Me best cow, too!"

The inspector chuckled and rattled his inspection form on a clipboard. Busha suddenly grew sombre: a form in the hands of a socialist was as bad as a gun. This inspector was a holdover socialist from the previous government, a man who took perverse delight in inflicting the intricacies of government documentaries on the lives of innocent citizens. The form would no doubt ask imponderable, insensible questions about everything under the sun – one could never anticipate or tell what a government form might ask – and all because every now and again Busha slaughtered one or two head of cattle on this spot.

Busha shuddered, awaiting the hoof in the face.

"Might as well begin, eh?" Busha said bravely.

"I already start," the inspector murmured.

Chapter Ten

Now came riding time. Riding morning, noon and night for the next week. Riding up mountain and down mountain, riding along the seacoast road, riding on a marl-stone lane that trickled through the bushland.

Riding began in the morning with the first light over the mountain tops and continued through the blazing noon sun when even John Crows knew better than to stay out in the heat, when donkey hood drop and school children leave the playground and seek the cool of a shade tree, when parsons will bury no dead body and fish will take no bait. But the German woman was oblivious to the sun, heat, hot wind, rough road. All she knew was riding, riding, riding.

And it was the worst kind of riding they did, too – on a hot motorcycle the German had rented. Its exhausts glowed like a stovepipe in the heat and fumes swirled up in the hot dry air and burned their noses. Yet the German woman still continued to ride.

On the first day of the riding Aloysius took her up into the mountains, through the villages of Walker's Wood, Lydford, Beechamville, Trafalgar, and Epworth – places he knew well because he had been hungry in them, or cut and bruised, or hurt.

The land in these places is like a still sea of green pastures and hills. It seeps over hummock and knoll into grasslands, and swirls into gullies, puddles into silent empty clearings where cows and goats graze in the Undertaker's wind that blows off the mountains every afternoon making the trees tremble.

She took pictures and remarked often that the land was the most beautiful she had seen, to which Aloysius always replied with dour memories: here was a tree under which he had once huddled against a driving rain, where he had sat drenched and frightened of the lightning and thunder through a long fretful night. There was a pasture where he used to sleep once, a long time ago, before the bushes drove him away with nasty gossip about his personal habits. At the foot of that mountain he had once spent a hungry week, his belly bawling every night for meat when he was only able to feed it wild fruit.

The woman saw none of these things. She saw only trees and green pastures and a mountain framed in a serene pose against the sky. She felt the wind and the sun on her cheek, and she saw none of the misery and pain in the empty land.

"Beautiful," she cried to a lovely wind-blown pasture.

Aloysius grunted.

The camera clicked like an insect outside one's window on a dark, dark night.

But after that first day he was a stranger to the land. She took him to places he had never seen. The motorcycle climbed hills he had never climbed, puttered down roads he had never walked. It drove through the hearts of towns and villages he had never even heard about, and everywhere they rode people stopped and turned to openly stare at the stout white woman and hairy black man on the rented motorcycle.

Aloysius knew his land the way a poor man knows it – the way a dog knows a bone, an infant its mother's breasts. But Aloysius did not know Jamaica the way the white woman knew her.

She knew the land the way a teacher knows a schoolbook. She knew history, lore, nomenclature – this last being one of the madman's thousand names, yet it also described how the woman knew Jamaica. The land was not her birthplace, not her homeland, was not a place that she loved – still she knew it better than Aloysius to whom the land had given life. It was a way of knowing that galled Aloysius so that he could hardly stand to talk with her and be told about the country, about the names of the mountains and villages and towns, about the names of parishes and places where long ago events of great importance had occurred.

One day she took him to a rugged cliff overlooking the sea and she told him that a long time ago a fierce battle had been fought between the English and the Spaniards here over possession of Jamaica. She showed him where the ships had lain at anchor and where the Spaniards had built fortifications against attack.

Now the ships were gone and the sea was empty in the heat of the sun and the fortifications were nothing more than an overgrown bushy ridge.

They walked over the bare land and wild macca bushes scratched at their ankles while the woman took photographs. Aloysius poked at the undergrowth with his foot looking for the bones of a dead soldier. But the soldiers who had died here had been dead so long that nothing at all remained of them. The wind soughed through the trees and a bird sang over this graveyard that looked like any other hillside, and there were no bones to be found anywhere.

"In de dark," Aloysius sobbed aloud, "me mind in de darkness."

"Vhat? Vhat you go on about now?" she wondered.

"De darkness cover me mind and me eye," he sobbed, rubbing his eyes as though to erase the darkness inside his mind.

"Dark? Is broad daylight dis. What de madman saying?" asked a bush.

"Maybe him blind," another whispered.

"Vhat darkness?" the woman grated impatiently.

"De darkness o' everlasting ignorance," Aloysius sobbed.

"You should be in German opera," the woman said without pity.

She lit a Sinsemilla joint.

"Broad rass daylight and negar man complain 'bout darkness," a bush hissed. "Ole negar never satisfy. God sun no good enough for dem. Now dey want lamp post and floodlight in broad daylight."

The German took a drag and cast her eyes over the empty landscape: the domination of macca bush and knotted undergrowth; the tangled vegetation so green and lush that it seemed blurry to the naked eye.

"History is shit," she grunted.

Yet Aloysius became so puffed up with the new knowledge he had gotten from the woman about Jamaica that he began to give lessons in geography to the flame heart tree. Sometimes the lessons lasted late into the night after the moon had already set behind the mountain and only the dim light of the stars fell on the darkened countryside.

"Jamaica," Aloysius told the tree after another wearying day of riding, "have 4,244 square miles."

"Eh, eh?" the tree marvelled.

"146 mile long and 51 wide. In de widest part."

"Of course," echoed the tree respectfully.

"120 river and stream run over dis island."

"Bumbo house!"

"30 million years ago dis island come outta de sea."

"What a long time!"

"Two thirds o' de island covered with limestone."

"Me never know stone come from lime."

Aloysius chuckled.

"No, man," he corrected. "Limestone is like marl stone."

"So where dis limestone come from?"

"Dead animal."

"Dead animal?"

"Dead snail. Dead crab. Dead crustaceans."

"Say what? Dead what?"

"Dead crustaceans. De little sea animal dem. When dey dead, dey leave behind a little pile o' bones. Dat what dem call limestone."

"Why dem don't call it crustacean stone?"

"Me don't know. So dey call it."

"So den all Jamaica is like one rass big graveyard? All day long we walk and talk 'pon top o' dead animals. No wonder dere so much parson in poor Jamaica."

"Is true, you know. Parson love a graveyard more dan crow love dead body."

But even an innocent conversation like this, overheard by bushes, became a dangerous thing. For the next morning Aloysius was awakened by a screeching bush.

"Repent, O crustaceans," the bush was raving, "for you soon dead and come to Jamaica. Dey goin' drive motorcar 'pon you head and school pickney dem goin' play cricket on you

Mumma jawbone. Den everybody – government minister and madman put together – goin' wee-wee 'pon you nose bridge. Dey goin' wee-wee 'pon you so much dey goin' make you fart!"

"Hush you rass!" Aloysius screamed.

The flame heart tree stirred.

"Morning, Aloysius," the tree said.

"Everybody love preach in Jamaica," Aloysius grumbled, settling back down on the ground. "Dat what wrong wid Jamaica. Too much rass preaching."

"Bee, you bumbo!" yelled the tree. "Move you rass. Is too early for pollination!"

"Preaching from ignorance," Aloysius mumbled sleepily. "As if crustacean have nose bridge."

"Rass negar bee grind me blossom before de sun even rise!" the tree yelped. "Bee, you blood!"

Riding was like reading. Or so it seemed to Aloysius in this week of constant, everlasting, never-ending riding on the pillion seat of the motorcycle clinging to the sweaty back of the thick white woman who had the map and decided on which roads to take. Even though Aloysius could not read, yet riding through the land was like reading it, was like seeing the story of the land and her people flash past one's eyes like the words of the book were said to march past the eyes of the comprehending reader.

A new day's journey was like the new page of a book. You could not say what lay around the next bend, or where the twisting road that slithered down the mountain would lead, whether into the hush of an overgrown valley or the openness of a canepiece with the sun glittering against the distant sea. You could not say how a road would come out or where it would end.

But each parish was like a separate chapter in the book of Jamaica. In Portland you could read stupor and contentment in the land where rain fell morning, noon and night, where bushes and trees rioted over the banks of mountains and dripped down the sides of hills in lush thickness. The people were poor but the bellies did not hang off the children because the sea was rich with fish and there were many rivers where shrimp and janga lived and could be caught by hand.

In St. Thomas the land became mountainous and sparse, the bushes thinning out and the rocky landscape protruding through the scrub like an old man's bones. Here was a land where the rain was not plentiful, a dry and arid parish loved by weeds and goats. Here you saw swollen bellies on the bodies of innocent children who stood by the roadside and stared at the passing motorcycle. Here the dry river beds cracked and fissured like old sores and the dust of the parched land billowed in the wake of the motorcycle.

At the end of each day's journey Aloysius would return to the foot of the flame heart tree and tell what he had read of the book of Jamaica.

"Today, we ride through the parish of Clarendon," he would tell the tree, settling against its trunk for an evening of quiet talk before sleeping.

"You think negar life hard?" the tree grumbled. "You should be a tree, if you want see hard life."

"Everybody life hard now and den."

"Don't chat no foolishness in me ear, sah! You ride 'round de whole island wid mad white woman. Me sit here all day in the hot sun giving grind to nasty negar bee. What me hear all day long? One donkey braying, dat's what! Who life harder?"

"Yours, sah. You have de harder life."

"A-hoa."

Aloysius understood that the tree was jealous, so he did not dispute with it. It would grumble for a few minutes then it would be eager to hear about Clarendon.

"So what 'bout Clarendon, now?" the tree finally asked.

Aloysius shared what he had seen in the land during a day of riding.

The woman gave him money. Aloysius did not ask her outright for money, but she understood his needs and gave it to him daily. He bought warm meals from roadside ramshackle shops where he was served rice and peas, curry goat, and plantain by a suspicious woman whose husband sat on a bar stool against a corner of the wattle-wall shack and stared while Aloysius ate his meals with a tablespoon in a dark corner.

Sometimes the German woman even ate with him. She abandoned the beautiful pink hotel that sat contentedly on the beach with every room gaping an open terrace at the cool breezes from the sea, and she rode with him to one of the food shacks tilting on the roadside and ate sitting beside him on a greasy table in the dark corner. But whenever she went with him the eyes craned to stare at the two of them: passers-by paused to flick glances into the shack at the stout white woman and the hairy madman. The proprietor and his woman peered at them from the dark doorway leading to the kitchen where a wood fire flickered red against a wall.

One night while Aloysius had stepped outside to relieve himself the proprietor hurried over to the dirty table in the corner where the woman sat alone and whispered urgently to her:

"Missus! Missus! You know dat man you wid is a madman?"

She recoiled with mock alarm.

"Mad?"

"Yes, Missus. He mad as mad can be. Him is a very dangerous man, Missus."

The woman laughed.

"That's all right. I mad too."

The man stared at her with bewilderment.

Then he chuckled.

"No, Missus. Don't say dat. White people don't go mad in Jamaica. Only negar go mad here."

"I say, I mad, too."

"You make joke 'bout dis, Missus. But is no joke. Him is a real madman."

"I say I mad, too. Listen to this."

The shopkeeper stared at her with wonder while she screwed up her face and took a deep breath like a small child struggling to inflate a new balloon.

"BUMBO! BUMBO! BUMBO! BUMBO CLAAT! BUMBO HOLE! BUMBO TOWN! BUMBO HEAD! BUMBO ISLAND! BUMBO WORLD! BUMBO BUMBO! EVERYTHING BUMBO!"

The man's mouth drooped open. Never in his born days had bumbo flown so freely in his presence. He could not believe his ears. Then he blinked as if he could not believe his eyes either.

Bumbo was a violent patois curse. In the Jamaican consciousness, bumbo lives under a damp rock like a poisonous lizard. Bumbo did not draw clean breath, show itself in the sunlight, or walk on lighted streets. Bumbo wrapped itself like a worm around the stem in the netherland of the brain where it grew fat and slimy on a diet of impiety and taboo.

The shopkeeper gasped like one violently slapped in the face. Bumbo hit him on the side of the head, on the chin; bumbo drove a dirty blade into the solar plexus of his dignity, manhood, conscience. His eyes gaped in astonishment: here in his establishment, a place of grit and decency, bumbo darted through the room like a rabid bat.

It was true that his shop was poor, that it resembled a weed growing out of the mud rather than a thing made by a human hand. Its floor was filthy. Flies swarmed everywhere in the dark room. Dim light trickled from a few kerosene lamps placed on the crude tables.

But poor might be dirty and poor might be ramshackle and stink like fat Queen Victoria after eight hours in a crinoline, but poor was not nasty. Bumbo was nasty.

The man drew himself up to a terrifying height. His wife flew to his side clutching a stick, ready to battle the benighted influence of Bumbo.

Aloysius sauntered back into the room.

"Listen me, Aloysius!" the proprietor told him angrily. "You is a madman because God mek you so. As long as you don't work you madness in me shop you is welcome. But dis woman not goin' put her foot cross my doorstep again. Get her out of me shop!"

The white woman laughed and stood up.

"Come, Aloysius," she cackled, "ve go. He doesn't like me."

At the doorway she turned.

"BUMBO!" she spat at the proprietor and his woman who stood stock-still in the same place over the dirty table.

The force of the bumbo brushed them back like a blast from an engine.

Then Aloysius and the woman were alone on the quiet street, walking towards where they had left the motorcycle under a tree, a knot of people peering out of the shop silently after them.

"You can't shout 'bumbo' to people in Jamaica, you know, man," Aloysius whispered to the woman as they mounted the motorcycle.

"Vhat does the vord mean?"

"Bad word. Bad bad word. You can't just come up to people in Jamaica and say bumbo. It don't work so."

"But *vhat* meaning has this vord?"

"Is a wicked word. You can't use dat word to people in Jamaica."

The woman laughed shrilly. She threw back her head and shrieked.

"BUMBO!"

The spectators in the doorway of the shop winced as one.

"Bumbo!" whispered one bush to another. "You hear dat?"

"Yes, sah. Foreigner come loosen 'bumbo' 'pon poor Jamaica. What is dis trial and tribulation now?"

The motorcycle roared off into the night. With the night breeze blowing past his ears, Aloysius tried to think about how to explain bumbo to the white woman. But the words would not come and the explanation that was clear to him he could not impart to a foreigner.

In the week of riding Aloysius gained weight from good eating and began to fart regularly like a rich man. Not only was he eating meat every day and drinking beverage, he was also getting a grind regularly from the woman, and the pum-pum was fattening him up and making him content. Even though he still woke up in the morning on the bare ground under the complaining flame heart tree with bushes babbling foolishness in his ear, he could not help waking up in the good mood of a parson on a Sunday morning. He awoke humming tunes and jumped up off his back like a whore on holiday.

But then something happened and the week of riding was abruptly over.

This was when things changed between them.

Chapter Eleven

A cultivator in a small village in St. Elizabeth went to bed early one night after a hard day of planting yam in the hot sun, and instead of sleeping and resting his weary bones, he waited up for late night pum-pum. His head was hurting him and his back was stiff from hoeing all day, but when his woman lay down on the bed beside him, he was convinced that he needed a grind. The next thing you know the tired hood and weary pum-pum had locked and he and the woman were fastened.

They grunted and struggled to get unfastened in the small room which was as black as pitch, this being an un-electrified district of St. Elizabeth, but it was no used. The hood was locked up inside the pum-pum like a rat in the belly of a snake. The woman bawled and cried for her mother and cursed the day she first laid eyes on hood; the farmer swore that if he could get unfastened he'd read Deuteronomy to his hood from now on every time it stood up. But no matter how they ranted and raved the hood was fastened inside the pum-pum and it wouldn't pop loose for love or money.

The next morning all the village knew: from the postmistress down to the teacher and the dressmaker – everybody had found out that the cultivator and his woman were fastened. The two of them were the laughing stock of the town as they were loaded into the back of a stake-body truck and driven to the hospital.

There the brown nurses and doctors jeered at them.

"I don't know why negar fasten so," one of the brown doctors told them. "Negar fasten more dan dog. Every week dem bring another negar dat fasten. You people take dis thing for a joke! You think I don't have nothing better to do wid me time dan unfasten grinding negar, eh?"

Then three of the nurses and attendants gripped the woman by the arms and around the waist, and another three took hold of the man. Both sides drew a breath and began to play tug-of-war with them.

The brown doctor stood between the two teams, yelling, "Pull, you rass! Pull! Pull!"

"Bumbo, boy," one of the men panted. "Dis hood cement."

Eventually, after much yelling and screaming, there was a loud pop and the teams sprawled backwards on the floor.

"Rass," the cultivator wailed, "me hood pop off! Piece of me hood pop off."

"Bumbo!" the woman screeched. "Me pum-pum plug!"

"Shut up you mouth!" the doctor scolded. "You don't see pop yet. You don't know what name plug yet. You soon see pop and plug."

"Pop and plug," said the flame heart tree, when Aloysius had paused in telling the story. "One good thing 'bout bee grind. Bee don't pop and plug nothing."

"De man pop, de woman plug. One brown man tell me it was in de *Star*," Aloysius moaned. "Dat's what I try to tell dis mad woman. One day we goin' fasten. All she want is hood, hood, hood."

This was the vexing worry presently between them.

Grinding was all the German woman wanted to do: grind morning, noon, and night in new spots. Old spot would not do anymore. If they had already had a grind under a tamarind tree, then they had to find another kind of tree to grind under the next time. If yesterday they caught a grind on an embankment, the next time they had to do it in a hollow or a gully. Once on a hillside, never again on a hillside. Always a new spot. Sometimes they had to walk miles into the bush just so they could find one.

"Why spot must be new?" Aloysius complained after an exhausting trek into the bush looking for a special new spot.

"I vant to do it everyplace in Jamaica on my holiday. I vant to do it in a gully."

"Sand will get inna me batty."

"Also, I vant to do it under a stop sign."

"Dat is out of order. You can't grind under stop sign in Jamaica. Dat's why de sign say stop. It means everything must stop. Even grinding."

"One night ve can find a stop sign and do it there. Vhat's the harm?"

"Me modder don't raise me to grind under stop sign! Dat is slackness!"

"Ve can do it also in a river."

"Make shrimp bite me hood?"

"And in the sea."

"Too much bumbo barracuda."

"Then ve can climb a tree, too. That vould be a new experience."

"Only monkey grind inna tree."

The German was demented about this grinding every time in a new place. So every day they walked to find a new spot, a place that suited her fancy, and then she gave him the pum-pum in that new place.

The woman did not understand that too much pum-pum can kill a man.

There was this man, for instance, a cabinetmaker from the district of Look-Behind in St. Elizabeth, an elder in his church, a faithful son who cared for his old mother and took old-fashioned pride in his workmanship: pum-pum killed him stone dead.

He married a slack half-Chinese girl from Westmoreland who insisted on giving him pum-pum every livelong day of his life. The cabinetmaker would come home after a hard day in the shop and the woman would give him the pum-pum. Sometimes he would beg her to stop, saying, "Lawd, me love! No bodder wid pum-pum tonight. Me too weak."

But she would laugh wickedly and reply, "Little pum-pum never hurt nobody."

Nothing the cabinetmaker did or said made a difference: every night of his life the woman gave him a dose of pum-pum. One evening he hid in the church to get away from her, but she tracked him down and dosed him with pum-pum right there in the pews.

Sometimes after he'd had a hard day at the shop she gave him nothing but pum-pum for his supper.

"What is dis on me poor head, Lawd Jesus," the poor man moaned to the Almighty. "Morning, noon and night nothing but pum-pum. Pum-pum here, pum-pum dere, pum-pum everywhere. Pum-pum more plentiful dan fish in de sea, dan mango in season. Pum-pum fall 'pon me head like heavy rain. What is dis tribulation on poor, poor me, O Lawd?"

The next day the cabinetmaker dropped dead in his shop as he worked to repair a mahogany what-not.

"Dis man overdose wid pum-pum," the District Medical Officer said, examining the body. "Look how him head swell, him belly pop out, him toe shrivel up like chicken foot. Only one thing cause dat: pum-pum overdose."

When Aloysius told the German woman that story and twenty others like it she would only laugh – everything was a big joke. He could swear that he'd heard that story from a man who used to know the cabinetmaker, who had attended the funeral, but it made no difference. Everything was a joke to her. No matter how serious he tried to be, she would only laugh and write down his words in her book.

One night of rain and lightning and thunder she took him to a rum bar and got him drunk. She bought him one white rum after another, and when he was thoroughly drunk, she suggested that they go to her hotel.

So they went. Aloysius warned her that if the manager saw them going into the hotel room together, he would make a fuss. The woman insisted. It was her room, she said, she paid rent for it every day. She could take anybody in her room that she wanted to. Even a donkey.

Why would she want to take a donkey into her room? What would she do to the poor beast?

She didn't want to take a donkey into the room, but she could take one if she wanted to, and that was the point she was making. She had paid for the room and it was her right to have guests in it if she wanted to.

But why would she want a donkey for a guest?

"I don't vant a fucking donkey in my room," the woman bellowed in his ear over a clap of thunder. "You drive me crazy vith stupid questions. Shut up and let's go."

The thunder rumbled so loud that he could feel the sound trickling up from the pavement and through his shin bones.

They huddled under the awning of a shop. Lightning lit up the darkened town showing gutters churning with brown water, a mangy dog cringing under the overhanging roof of a bank, trees bent over in the moaning wind.

They dashed from shop to shop catching a quick shelter from the rain under the awnings and then racing again across the flooded streets.

Soon they were at the hotel. She ran through the back door and they made their way, dripping wet, up the dark back stairway, leaving a trail of water behind them in the dim hallway.

Then they were inside the room, and he was so frightened of it that he did not want to go in but stood just inside the door. He had seen rooms like this in magazines and at the pictures, but he'd never seen a room like this before with his own eyes.

It was a wonderful, rich room as silent and strong as a cave, but in a high place like a bird nest. Inside this room he could not hear the roar of the rain. Lightning could not harm it, and the thunder rumbled harmlessly in the background of the dark night like a faraway passing train. If he didn't look out of the window, he would not have known that rain was falling, so wonderful, strong and silent was this room.

The rum had confused his brain, and now the rich room made him feel bewildered and afraid.

He leaned against the wall and put his head in his hands and the woman asked him what was wrong, and he told her that the rum and room had confused his brain. She wondered how a room could confuse his brain, but when he tried to explain it to her, his head started to spin, so he leaned against the wall to catch his breath.

The German said she had an idea and wondered if he'd let her try a new thing tonight.

What was the new thing?

She wanted to tie him up in the bed and get a grind that way. The new thing: grinding a tied up Jamaican madman on a bed during a storm. Perhaps no woman in the world had ever done such a thing before. For when you thought about it, was it likely that ever before in the history of womankind, a German woman had tied up a Jamaican black madman on a bed in an American hotel and fucked him senseless right there and then during a storm?

Tie up? Why must the man be tied up? Assuming, for the sake of argument, that there was a madman in the room right now, why can't German woman give such a person a grind untied on the bed?

"Every idea I have is a bad idea," she raged. "Vhat is wrong with you? Vhat's bad about a harmless idea like dis?"

He didn't like the part about tie up, dat's all. That was the only part he didn't like.

But the rum and the room and the woman ganged up on him, and before he had sense enough to say no and run, the woman had talked him over to the bed and laid him out spread-eagled on the sheets and tied him up hands and feet on its four bed-corners.

At first he thought it was a joke to be so tied up, but after she had finished with the tying and he tried to move his arms or wriggle the rope off his foot, he realized that she well knew how to tie up a man for no matter how he squirmed or twisted there was no escaping.

She went into the bathroom and left him bound to the bed and he tried to pass it off as a good laugh by remarking in a loud voice that she definitely had a wonderful way of tying up a man on a bed so that no matter how hard he struggled he couldn't get away, but now that she'd proven that a woman could tie up a man like a chicken, he would like her please to release him because he didn't want to be tied up anymore. He didn't realize how loud he was talking until he heard his own voice.

The woman came slowly out of the bathroom. She walked into the room not like a woman in ordinary life, but like one in the pictures.

She took off her clothes deliberately, a wicked look in her eye.

"Me don't like dis tie up business, Inga," he whined as she approached the bed. "Make me untie before we do de rudeness."

She chuckled.

Then it all became clear: the reason why she had tied him up, why she walked into the room so funny.

He remembered a horrible movie he had seen only months ago at the Roxy. There was a white woman in it who walked funny and had sharp teeth. She took a white man who sold bibles door-to-door for a living into her room and tied him up on her bed. He wriggled and bawled for mercy. But she had no mercy. She just tilted back his head and sucked blood out of his neck until only a limp sheet of skin was left of him.

It hit Aloysius like blinding revelation hits a Pentecostal.

"BUMBO!" he shrieked. "HELP! MURDER! NECKSUCK!"

"Vhat are you doing!" she hissed, rushing over to the bed.

"MURDER TO RASS!" he bellowed, hurling himself up and down on the bed so hard that, even tied up hand and foot, he still caused the springs to pound against the wall.

The woman was on him like a flash. She straddled his struggling form and practically spat in his eye, "Shut up!" which so terrified him that he screamed even louder.

She grabbed a pillow and tried to smother his screams under it. With a ferocious heave, he flung her off the bed and redoubled his shrieking.

She sprang back on top of him, pushed the pillow down over his head and pressed down on it with her elbows.

There was a furious knocking on the door. The woman rushed into the bathroom just before the brown-skin night manager opened the door and walked into the room.

Aloysius sobbed his story as the manager struggled to untie him.

"She tie me up on de bed, sah, and was going suck me neck. Just like date de woman in *Vampire Woman* do to de Bible salesman at de Roxy. She was going suck me neck, sah, when you walk in."

"I can't untie dese damn knots," the manager snapped.

"Ve are lovers," the German said haughtily, clutching a bathrobe around her, "that is all there is to it! Ve vere going to make love before you crashed in here."

"You and dis man is lovers! Dis is a madman! How you can love a madman?" the manager asked with astonishment.

"Is lie, sah!" Aloysius blubbered. "Is me neck she was goin' suck, sah. Next morning de maid find nothing but a body husk on de bed. All blood suck out."

"He's lying. Here, get out of my way and I'll untie him," the German said.

"BUMBO! NO MAKE HER KILL ME, SAH!" Aloysius bawled, while the woman fumbled with the ropes.

"Hush up you mouth. She not goin' trouble you."

A maid peeped around the open door from the hallway.

"What happen, Missah Jones?" she asked timidly.

"No dis white woman here tie up madman on de bed."

"To suck blood outta me neck," Aloysius sobbed.

"Tie up madman?" the maid asked, coming cautiously into the room. "Oh, is no Aloysius dat! Aloysius, what happen to you?"

"De woman want suck me neck! She tie me up on de bed like chicken. Me bawl when me see what she want do! Thank God dat Missah Manager come in and save me, odderwise is nothing but husk left fe you find inna morning."

The German finished untying the knots and Aloysius sprang off the bed.

"Thank you, sah! Thank you very much!"

"I want both o' you outta me hotel right now!" the manager snapped.

"Vhy you tell him this lie?"

"You tie me up and frighten me!" Aloysius mumbled with shame. "Why you must tie me up, for? Why everything must always be new?"

"I don't know which one of you is de madder one. But me want both of you outta dis place tonight! Melba, go call de Special Constable downstairs."

The maid left the room.

"Lawd, sah, beg you," Aloysius whined. "No call policeman on me, sah. Me not giving no trouble, sah."

"What a damn nerve, eh?" The manager fumed. "A foreign woman come to Jamaica and tie up a local madman on a bed in dis hotel on my shift! You like to tie up madman? Why you don't go to de madhouse in Kingston? Dey got whole heap o' madman dere you can tie up! Why you must come tie one up in my hotel? Damn out of order!"

"Get out of my room so I can pack my suitcase," the German said frostily.

"If you never tie me up, me wouldn't say nothing," Aloysius muttered. "Me think is me neck you want suck."

"Out of dis hotel in five minutes or I goin' get de Special Constable to carry you rass to jail!" the manager raged, slamming the door as he left.

While the woman packed her suitcase Aloysius followed her around the rich room apologizing and trying to explain.

The two of them were standing in front of the hotel five minutes later.

The storm had rumbled out to sea. In its wake it had left a clammy, hazy night. A damp breeze brushed their faces. Dark, wet streets shone under the streetlights.

"Vell," the German chuckled. "After this, there is only one thing for me to do."

"What dat?"

"Go and stay in the bush vith you."

And that was how this foreign woman ended up living in the bushland of St. Ann, a parish having more parson than mongoose but only one rich man: Busha McIntosh.

BOOK II

Chapter Twelve

From afar on a dark night the house of Busha McIntosh looked like a ship at sea. Fluorescent lights the colour of watery milk streamed through its open windows. Its generator made odd thumping noises so one would almost think the house was driven through the darkness by a powerful engine. When Busha entertained guests, as he did tonight, the sounds of their laughter drifted deep into the night.

Come daylight, Busha's house did not cry out for a second look. One saw no conspicuous richness in it; one saw only a scruffy driveway cut into the hillside that tethered the house to the land like a leash on an expensive dog.

But if you were a poor man walking past Busha's house at night you could not help but see the glow of light it cast over the darkened grounds and wonder: you could not help but look up at this wonderful house and dream about living with your loved ones on such a mountaintop.

From the foot of the tree where she now stayed with Aloysius, Inga could also see the house shining on the hill.

"Who is that man that lives in that house," she wondered on her second night.

"Dat Busha McIntosh house," Aloysius said. "Busha own all dis land. Dis is government land we living on, but Busha own all de odder land around us."

"Vhy one man owns all this?"

"Why tree can't walk? Why tree must stand in one spot and give bee grind all day?" the tree mimicked the woman.

The tree had taken an instant and jealous dislike to her.

"Busha own dis land as long as me live. From me is a little boy, Busha own all dis land," Aloysius explained.

"A fat man, I suppose?"

Aloysius chuckled.

"Busha have a good belly on him."

"A fat pig," Inga grunted. "All this land he owns. And there he lives on top of a hill in a big house."

"Busha born wid silver spoon in him mouth."

"I notice two things about rich people. No matter where I go, I notice these two things. First, they always build their houses on hills. I never see a rich man house on bottom land. Always high up, like a bird."

"Everybody love cool breeze," Aloysius muttered.

"I notice too that a rich man is usually a fat one. I never in my life see a thin rich man."

"Everybody love deir belly."

"What you bring dis rass woman here for, eh, sah?" the tree scolded Aloysius for the hundredth time. "She just come chat a bunch of foolishness in me ears. Why you have to bring dis rass woman in de bushland to come trouble me peace o' mind?"

"She not troubling you."

"Vhat? Vhat he say about me now?"

"Nothing. Him don't say nothing."

Already there were bitter feelings between the woman and the tree.

"He said something about me. I'll shut him up."

The woman pulled off her pants and panties, squatted down to open her legs, and pissed on the tree.

The tree screeched.

"Bumbo hole! It tickle! No piss 'pon me root! Dat tickle!"

She pissed like a horse: a jet of water spurted from between her legs and trickled in slow fingers over the roots of the tree.

"Lawd, Inga!" Aloysius begged. "Him don't like dat!"

To add insult to injury, she shook the pum-pum cruelly at the tree's trunk, then shone it like a flashlight in Aloysius's face. The hood rose immediately.

"No grind in front o' me! Blood! No grind in front o' me!" the tree bellowed.

But it was too late. She waddled towards Aloysius, the pants coiled around her ankles scraping dust off the ground.

"Bumbo!" the tree screeched.

Only two days now the woman had been in the bushland but already there was not a minute's peace.

"I'm going to tell you how human nature go. You want to hear how it go?" Busha was asking his guests in the drawing room.

Three men were in the room, each clutching a rum glass and feeling content with life, and not a one particularly interested in Busha's view of human nature. A breeze wafted through the windows thrown open to catch the night air, bringing into the room the hums and wails of insects in the bushland darkness.

One of the men was Parson Mordecai, a bowler on the cricket side who delivered the cricket ball with subtle bounces that mystified batsmen. Ambitious and determined to make bishop before he turned fifty, the parson was renowned throughout the parish for his fiery sermons against rum and pum-pum. One Sunday he would blast rum from the pulpit with hell-fire and brimstone; the next, he would lambaste pum-pum. Sometimes he would do a double-header and bawl out against both of them. He called rum and pum-pum the Devil's Tweedle-dum and Tweedle-dee. If Tweedle-dum don't get you, he would roar from the pulpit at the subdued men in his congregation, Tweedle-dee would.

During these sermons the suffering possessors of Tweedle-dee would sit silent and scolding beside their men, occasionally casting them tight-lipped glares and nodding in grim agreement with the parson: Too much damn Tweedle-dee, their sour faces said – that's all worthless Jamaican men wanted.

The rum juice was sitting sweet inside his belly like a banked fire, and the parson was feeling wonderful about himself and the world. He did not give a whit about the Busha's views of human nature. Besides, the Busha had the same views on human nature to express at every meeting, and the parson had already heard them.

Another of the men was a Doctor Fox, treasurer of the cricket team and its opening batsman. Five years from now he had been settled in the parish of St. Ann.

Nicknamed Dr. Head Or Toe by the village men, this doctor loved to examine a pum-pum more than puss love to torment mouse. It had got so bad that none of the village men would allow their women to go to him unless it involved a wound either to the head or the toe – parts so indubitably distant from what a woman carried between her legs that even this rude doctor could not use scrapes and bruises to those extremities as an excuse for poking around in her private parts.

He too was not interested in Busha's opinions on human nature. He sipped his rum and stared morosely out the window, where darkness banked thick against a bougainvillea bush, and wished Busha would shut up about human nature.

The third man sat in a chair in the far corner, his head hidden in the shadows. He was Inspector Williams of the village constabulary, the wicket keep of the cricket side. In the dim light of the room his belly folded over his belt and bulged out under his shirt like a smooth roll of kneaded dough.

The inspector was wondering where Busha's wife was, for he was rather fond of the poor woman. Her batty was as big and firm as the hump on a camel, and obviously the Busha was not doing the job properly. The inspector could tell. He had only to look at a woman's face to tell whether or not she was being properly ploughed. Busha's wife clearly was underplanted. Her husband was too much taken up during the daytime hours with stupidness such as butchering cows and cultivating guinea grass while right under his nose the field that most badly needed ploughing languished beside him on the bed at night worrying if there was life after death.

The inspector stirred and wondered where the suffering woman was at this very moment. No doubt she was someplace in a dark back room peering out at the stars and wishing she was a firefly.

The men were gathered in Busha's drawing room to select a cricket side for the upcoming match against Walker's Wood. The last match had been an ignominious defeat for Moneague and revenge was on the committee's mind. But then the business about the lunatic Aloysius had come up, and the fact that a white woman – obviously a nasty and insensible foreigner – was living in the bushland with him was mentioned, to which every man present had delivered a strong opinion.

The parson was of a mind that Tweedle-dee had struck again – this time a helpless madman was in its virile grip. He speculated about the heinousness of foreigners in general who came to innocent islands such as Jamaica and spread moral turpitude all over the land, like, he said – lapsing regrettably into pulpit phraseology – cow dung. Not even a Jamaican madman was safe from these wicked women, the parson sighed, and God knew that if a madman who lived like a harmless hermit in the bush wasn't safe from the clutches of a foreign temptress, then no man, not even a Pope, was safe.

It reminded him, the parson opined, of Aeschylus's view of human life: "Count no man safe this side of the grave."

The doctor thought the parson's opinion was a damn load of foolishness and more or less said so. The inspector agreed that enough was enough, and the parson should save his rubbish for Sunday congregations. Even Busha guffawed at the parson's words.

The thing about it all, said Busha, was that the foreign woman was probably overcome when she saw the size of Aloysius's hood. The man had a hood on him as big as any bull. In fact, Busha was convinced that big hood and socialism were responsible for driving Aloysius mad. When you thought about it, the poor lunatic was walking around with two pounds of hood dangling between his legs, pulling him down. Add to this the torment of socialism, speculated Busha, as practised in the last eight years by the previous government, and it was more than enough to drive any man mad.

"Don't you remember the time Aloysius went mad in the village and tear off all him clothes?" Busha asked. "It was during the budget debates, when the damn Prime Minister chat for eight hours non-stop. When Miss Lindsay the postmistress saw the size of his hood, she passed out in a dead faint right on de counter. Don't you remember that time?"

It was a little like a man walking around with a two-pound fish dangling off his crotch, Busha said. Think about it! Busha marvelled to the parson. Imagine if you had a two-pound snapper swinging like a cast-iron bell clapper off your crotch. (Busha had lately caught a two-pound yellow tail snapper off the coast of Ocho Rios and he appreciated that two pounds was a good weight.)

The parson didn't like the implication that a lowly madman in the bush had a bigger hood than a university educated parson, but at the same time he didn't want to come right out and defend the size of his own member.

"Some men have a two-pound snapper between them leg, Busha," the parson muttered ominously. "Other men have three-pound parrot fish."

"And odder men have four-ounce guppy," the inspector chuckled with a nasty belly-laugh.

The doctor was privately wishing that the woman would develop some kind of disease and come to him for treatment. To tell the truth, he wouldn't mind treating a white pum-pum for a change. It just got to be a bore handling black and brown and Chiny and Indian pum-pum day in and day out. Not that he objected to native pum-pum as the staple of his practice, but Lawd God man, every workman in the world craved a little variety in his daily labour.

What depressed the doctor was the unjust state of affairs in the island where a homeless lunatic was getting to grind white pum-pum every night while he, a licensed medical practitioner, had never examined one in real life. True, a white pum-pum was the same as a black one and the doctor knew that by heart: but it was only depressing textbook knowledge. The fact is that never in his born days had he ever seen a live white pum-pum. For that matter, not even a dead one.

He had been trained at the University of the West Indies, where even the cadavers had been black or brown because they were cheap and plentiful. You just didn't have that many white people living in Jamaica. And when a white woman did die, even one that was old and shrivelled up, her people were the quickest on the island to bury her in the deepest imaginable hole or tomb her up behind tons of solid concrete.

One time the Busha's wife had come to the doctor for treatment of an ear infection and when he'd told her to disrobe she asked him to his face if he was mad. The woman didn't understand that infections spread: many a female disease started in the ear then headed straight for the pum-pum. A germ was no fool. The doctor had even attempted a feeble joke about it to Mrs. Busha. "Ear today, pum-pum tomorrow," he'd cracked and very nearly been boxed for his wit.

For his part, the doctor said, he was certain the woman must have some venereal disease, which she would no doubt spread all over Jamaica. Don't think, he warned, that because the foreign woman was sleeping with a madman that the infection wouldn't spread. Next thing you knew, a parson would get it, then a government minister, and before you knew it, a foreign diplomat.

The parson got vexed at the implication that the disease would automatically spread from a madman to a man of the cloth. A row nearly started but for Busha's wife, who walked into the room and settled heavily on the couch.

"Tired of looking up at cloud and stars, eh, Sarah?" the inspector enquired with a sympathetic smirk.

"Looking at cloud?" she snapped. "Who looking at cloud? I was killing a chicken."

"Killing chicken?" the inspector guffawed. "Why you killing de poor chicken? De chicken trouble you?"

In his rum-clouded reasoning, the inspector was quite certain that she had just been torturing some hapless rooster in a back room – for symbolic reasons entirely lost on her stupid husband.

"De damn garden boy didn't kill the chicken we suppose to stew tomorrow. So I had to kill it meself. Dat's the way life in Jamaica go, don't you know? If you want to do anything, you have to do it yourself. It don't matter if you have three or four people working for you. It don't matter if you told de damn garden boy to kill the chicken from two days ago. If it was up to him, the chicken would live long enough to draw a government pension."

The men chuckled. The inspector's eyes burned with admiration. Sarah was sitting on a soft couch, and his eyes could appreciate the way her bountiful batty spread out and settled on top of the cushion in a neat, elliptical puddle. And right next to that wonderful batty, squinting cycloptically through the dim electric light that filtered through gabardine dress and cotton panties, was squeezed the tormented underploughed field.

"You want me to shoot him tomorrow?" Busha asked drunkenly.

When Busha got drunk he was willing to shoot anyone with whom his wife professed annoyance.

"Don't talk no foolishness in me ear, Hubert. You is in another world."

Busha denied that he was in another world. Just to demonstrate his physical presence, he lurched forward and planted a wet kiss on her brow, which she flicked off with an impatient palm.

"We were talking about dat madman who live in de bush," the inspector explained to Mrs. Busha. "He have a foreign woman living dere wid him now. What you think of dat, eh?"

Mrs. Busha didn't think much of it. She thought the madman ought to be immediately arrested and the woman deported. As far as she could see, for a madman who lived like an animal in the bush to suddenly find himself shacked up with a tourist woman only encouraged other men to go mad.

"Dat's why we must practise belly therapy at Bellevue!" the Busha explained to his wife, swaying giddily in the drawing room. "Dey used to feed de lunatics in Bellevue very good food! Some madman used to go dere just to get fat! But we changed dat when I was on de review board. I said to de doctor one day – an American named Dr. Brown. Anyway, one day he come and tell me that such-and-such a patient have Oedipus Complex. I said to him, What kind o' complex him have? Him say, Oedipus: him want to sleep with him modder. I said to dis doctor, Listen me here, I said, don't tell me 'bout ole negar in Jamaica want to do something to him modder and dat's why him in de madhouse! Is when him can't get to do it to him modder dat him go mad, not when him want do it! I say to him, When old negar want pum-pum ..."

"Lawd, Hubert!" Sarah chided.

"Sorry me love. This is man talk. I say to him, when ole negar want pum-pum, de first piece him can grab him grab! And it don't matter if it have foot to walk or if it fly or creep or live in hole in de ground, so long as it have pum-pum ..."

The men laughed.

Busha expanded like a bellows and weaved in and out of a shadow thrown by an overstuffed chair.

"Him say to me, de man need therapy. I say, you want to know what de best kind o' therapy is for Jamaica: belly therapy. You gone stark raving mad? Good: you don't get nothing to eat but belly wash and bread back. You stop you ranting and raving? Good: now you get a piece o' chicken batty and a

Johnny cake. You start acting like a decent human being? Good: now you get flour dumpling, chicken wing, and gravy. You tell me you want to work for a living? Good: now you get all de ackee and saltfish you can eat, all de rice and peas and plantain you belly can hold."

"Busha," the inspector chortled, "you should open a clinic in St. Ann."

"Him say to me dat I don't understand mental illness. I answer, but common sense tell me dat dere is no such thing as a hungry madman! When a man hungry, de belly bring back sanity. Is when de belly is full dat de mind have de time to go mad. Dat is why you have more madman in the United States dan on any odder country on de face o' de earth. Because de whole population over dere have a full belly!"

"Anyway," the doctor said, after the laughter had died down, "we still need Aloysius on de team."

Mrs. Busha hissed with contempt.

"Why you team can't win without a madman on it?"

"Aloysius is a good spin bowler," the doctor said.

"Plus, you know me dear," Busha added, "dere is nothing dat bring fear to a batsman heart quicker dan facing a mad bowler."

"Den what you should do, den," Mrs. Busha said disgustedly, "is go to Bellevue and draw eleven madman out for your side. Better yet, go to Parliament and get all de ministers to come bowl for you. For dem all mad. Den you bound to win. I going to me bed, Hubert. Good night all."

"Good night, Sarah," the inspector said, wetting his lips as she sauntered out of the room. "Remember, now. Despair is not de answer."

Mrs. Busha kissed her teeth at this cryptic comment and went into the kitchen to fix herself a cup of bedside cocoa and – in the inspector's opinion – take another vengeful and symbolic swat at the corpse of the dead rooster.

"Another round, gentlemen?" Busha asked, waving the rum bottle.

"Certainly, sah, certainly," the inspector seconded.

"Boy, dere is no way we must lose de match dis year," the doctor commented, holding out his own empty glass.

"One for de road," said the parson, standing up and stretching, filling the room with the sound of cracking middle-aged bone.

The meeting lasted late into the night. Four bottles of rum perished at its hands. A little strategy was discussed mixed in with a great deal of ribald gossip. But when it was over and the men stumbled into the dark night of the countryside, Busha had been charged the dual mission of finding out if Aloysius would consent to bowl for the village in the next cricket match, along with whatever else he could about the foreign woman now living in the bush with the lunatic.

Chapter Thirteen

Worries followed between Aloysius and Inga, one after another. Arguments, rows, quarrels over foolishness. Every night, pum-pum. Every morning, observations. Every afternoon, a walk in the bush. Every night, more observations. More rows. More pum-pum.

Observations: Inga constantly made observations about life in the bush. She wrote observations down in her book. She read them out to Aloysius and insisted that he agree with them. And when he did not, a bitter row ensued.

Listen to one of their arguments. She wrote down in her book that she understood now what had made the rich man callous and unfeeling about others worse off than himself: Hiding his doo-doo in plumbing pipes had made him a vain and uncaring wretch.

But in the bush there was no place to hide your doo-doo. It was there every morning where you had deposited it the day before, an incubator of swarming flies. The prosperous banker, on his way to work in his Mercedes, did not have to drive past his own pyramid of doo-doo perched on the curb. He did not perceive that this product of his most necessary bodily function was used by nature as a nursery for maggots. The same insight was lost on the movie starlet whose picture was in a magazine every week. If she was ruler of the world, Inga declared, she would pass a law that would force everyone to exhibit his doo-doo on his doorstep every day with a label attached identifying the name and address of its maker. Workers could go and see what their employer's bowels had introduced into the world today. The silent worshipper of a beautiful woman on a bus could follow her to her doorstep and cure his romantic feelings by prodding at her most recent pile with a stick. Men would not be so cocksure or women so vain. Pretence would be reduced throughout the world because doo-doo would tell the true story about everyone. That's why the rich man hid doo-doo in pipes. He did not want the whole story to come out.

Aloysius did not understand what story doo-doo told. He fretted that his thinking was too shallow to see even the meaning of doo-doo.

When he had lived alone he always made sure that he performed his bodily functions a great distance from where he slept and ate. Sometimes he went into a thickly wooded spot, although this usually started a fierce clamour of outrage among the bushes of, "Jesus God Almighty, why madman must come doo-doo here?" Sometimes he scouted out a deep gully. But he always did it far away from where he slept and ate.

But Inga was lazy in the morning. She liked to wake up and write and drink a hot drink. Immediately afterwards, she had an urgent bowel movement. The first morning she went only a few yards away, stooped down behind a bush, and did the ugly business there.

So the next day – since doo-doo doesn't take up foot and walk – the pile was still in the same place. And the woman saw it.

She was understandably disgusted and squeamish. But by the second day when she passed by the same bush again and saw her pile of doo-doo she had found philosophy in it. She flew from doo-doo to notepad and wrote furiously.

The next day she took another morning stroll past the doo-doo and examined it again, this time with many mutterings in her strange tongue.

That was when she told Aloysius about the law she would pass if she were ruler of the world.

"Already I learn something new from this experience," she told Aloysius. "It came to me this morning. I wrote down my thoughts about it. Shit has deep meaning."

Aloysius scowled.

"What dat mean, now?"

"Vell, it's simple," she said, settling down against the trunk of the tree. "You know, vhen you live in a house, vhen you live in a hotel, you do not really ever get to see your shit. Once you have made it, you flush it down the toilet and it becomes property of the municipal government. But vhen you have to go in the bush and every day you must see vhat you made a week ago, still decomposing and stinking, it tells you something important about you."

"Vhat dat?"

He suddenly realized to his dismay that he was saying his "w" like a "v" the way the woman did, and he became very vexed with himself for behaving like a follow-fashion monkey.

"What it say?" he repeated, elongating and emphasizing the "W."

"Vell, it says many things. It makes you realize that you and the dog in the street and the Queen on the throne and the Pope in the Vatican have this single thing in common: you must all take your daily shit, no matter vhat is your position in this world."

Aloysius balked.

"Foolishness," he declared, stirring impatiently.

"What dat she say now?" the tree asked.

"She say de Queen doo-doo every day, too."

The tree chuckled at the woman's denseness.

"You talking to me or the tree?" the woman asked angrily.

Aloysius laughted like a big-belly parson baptizing a sinner.

"Vhy you laugh?"

"Everybody know dat is not true."

"Vhat's not true? You don't think that the Queen must take her daily shit, too?"

"Queen don't do dat thing! Hi! You don't have no common sense?"

Her face turned an angry red.

"You trying to tell me that the Queen doesn't shit, you ignorant man?"

"De Queen is Queen of all de West Indian dominions!" said the tree huffily. "She is Empress of India and Monarch o' Pakistan. She is titular head o' we Commonwealth and mistress o' de ermine robe and keeper o' de great seal and de golden key. Dis is a woman born upon dis world in a special place o' glorified distinction. Dis is not you common trash out in de street! Dis is de Queen! How she going doo-doo? You is out of order!"

"Ignorant?" Aloysius replied scornfully. "Is me you call ignorant? Listen to dis woman," he appealed angrily to the tree. "She calling me ignorant. De pot call de kettle black!"

"Damn out of order!" grumbled the tree. "You think de Governor General o' Jamaica, Honorable Florizel Augustus Glasspole, who is representative o' her Imperial Majesty, you think he representing somebody who doo-doo every day? Foolishness!"

"You stupid lunatic! Everybody in this world shits! Everybody!"

"How you know dat? Tell me how you know dat?"

"You're trying to drive me mad like you are!" the woman screeched. "Tell me, does the Pope shit?"

"Me don't business wid Pope. But me know dat my Queen don't doo-doo. Learn dat! A-hoa!"

"You fool! I can't believe you actually think that! Everybody shits! Everybody!"

"You ever see my Queen doo-doo?" Aloysius challenged, standing his ground fearlessly.

"Of course not. But she is human too, just like you and me. She also must shit."

"But you never see her do it," pounced Aloysius, the barrister in him coming out in full force, "so how you know she do dat thing?"

"You ass!" the woman bellowed.

"Sticks and stones will break my bones," Aloysius chanted in the gloating tone of a vengeful schoolboy who has just won an argument.

The woman flew into a rage, grabbed a rock, and was about to bust his head with it in her uncontrollable fury when they heard the sounds of footsteps trampling through the underbrush.

"Aloysius!" a voice bellowed. "Aloysius! I want to see you."

They turned and saw Busha McIntosh clawing his way through the thicket and emerging into the clearing.

Busha had taken his charge seriously: recruit Aloysius for the cricket side and find out more about the white woman living in the bush with him. But then he'd gotten busy with butchering, foaling, and planting before the October rains. Three days had passed since the cricket committee had drunk rum and plotted strategy, and it was only today that Busha had remembered his responsibility.

This morning as he was driving past the stretch of land where Aloysius usually lived, Busha had had an impulse. He pulled over the Land Rover onto the shoulder of the road and tramped into the bush to find the lunatic.

It was only ten o'clock in the morning but already the sun was high over the rim of the mountain and licking sweat off Busha's florid face.

At the edge of the clearing he stood, mopping his flushed brow with a white handkerchief.

"Busha!" Aloysius gushed, rushing towards him in relief. "Busha. How you do, Busha?"

"All right, man, all right. How you?" Busha murmured, tramping towards Inga, who still glowered with murderous rage.

"Introduce me to you friend, Aloysius?" Busha said, smiling broadly.

"He is not my friend! He is an ignoramus!" the woman screeched.

"What?" Busha looked around uncertainly from one to the other. "I coming in on a fight?"

"He is stupid! Everybody shits! Everybody!"

Aloysius tried to take Busha aside, but Busha shrugged off the grimy paw on his arm and approached the woman gingerly.

Busha offered his hand.

"My name is Hubert McIntosh. But everybody call me Busha!"

Inga ignored the hand.

"My name is Inga Schmidt. And he is stupid!"

"Busha!" Aloysius pleaded. "Sorry, Busha. What you want see me 'bout, sah?"

In an urgent whisper, he added, "She have a temper, Busha. And we was in de middle o' deep argument. Is all right, Busha. Come over here, sah. What you want see me 'bout, sah?"

Aloysius tugged at Busha's arm and tried to lead him away from the woman.

But Busha was overcome by curiosity.

"You sound like a European," he said genially.

"I am German! I come from Berlin, if it's any of your business! Vhich it is not."

"Well, I'm sorry I caught you in such a bad mood," Busha mumbled.

"He thinks the Queen of England doesn't shit!" the woman screeched indignantly. "That's how stupid he is!"

"Who?" Busha retreated a step or two. "What's that?"

"He says the Queen doesn't shit like you and me!"

"Well, you see, Miss Schmidt," Busha tried to explain, flustered at being caught in the crossfire and dimly remembering some words and phrases that had been flogged into him as a schoolboy, "we are a small country without many hallowed institutions. The concept of our sovereign is so important to our way of thinking that the man in the street has a tendency to elevate the person who sits on the throne ..."

The woman looked provoked.

"You saying the Queen doesn't shit, too?"

"Not at all, not at all," Busha said soothingly. "I'm just trying to establish background, that's all. You see, what Aloysius no doubt meant ..."

"Does the Queen shit or doesn't she?" the woman barked.

Busha got his hackles up. An obdurate look hardened over his features like drying starch.

"No," he barked back. "She does not!"

Aloysius hurried to the woman's side.

"Inga," he pleaded. "No make such a fuss 'bout it with Busha. Is not Busha argument dis ..."

"VHAT?" the woman howled. "The Queen doesn't shit? You encourage his ignorance vhen you say that!"

"I'll thank you not to scream at me," Busha said coldly. "This is a free country, not your Nazi Germany. We're all entitled to our opinions here. And I for one am with Aloysius. Our Queen does not defecate. What's more, our Queen has never defecated, and would never stoop to defecate."

"You stupid Jamaican! Don't you shit?"

"Certainly not!" Busha retorted indignantly.

"BUMBO! SHIT! FUCK! PISS! FUCK! BUMBO! BUMBO! COCK!"

Inga shrieked this nastiness at the sky.

"Dis woman is even madder than you!" Busha muttered to Aloysius.

"It's people like you who have made him vhat he is," she hissed. "You tell him your lies and he believes them. You vant to know vhat I'm doing here vith him, don't you? That's vhy you come here, isn't it? To snoop and find out vhy I'm staying here vith him?"

"I don't care who you stay with," Busha said stoutly.

"I stay vith him because he has a big cock! Vhat you think of that?"

She was shrieking so loud that spittle began dribbling down the corners of her mouth.

"If you'll excuse me," Busha said with impressive dignity, "I have some business with Aloysius."

Talking quietly, Busha and Aloysius huddled in the middle of the clearing. The woman was in such a raging fury that she grabbed the tree trunk and bit it savagely, spitting out a great gob of bark.

"BUMBO!" the tree shrieked. "She bite me rass! Rass hole, she bite me rass."

"Lawd, Inga," Aoysius begged, rushing towards her. "No bite him, man. Him bawling."

"Jesus Christ," Busha muttered. "Dis is worse dan de madhouse."

Told the story that night at dinner of the row between Aloysius and the white woman, Sarah had decided opinions about it.

"Good for Aloysius," she declared, "standing up for our Queen."

"I think the woman is madder dan him," Busha muttered, gnawing on a chicken leg. "She bite a piece outta de tree just like you see me bite this leg."

"Where dese damn women come from nowadays, eh?" Sarah wondered rhetorically. "Where dey get dem from? Why would any decent woman want a dirty lunatic like Aloysius?"

Busha delicately paraphrased the comment that the woman had made about Aloysius's private parts.

"It must be dat she like," Sarah said with contempt.

She pushed away her plate.

"I'm so upset I can't eat."

"Why?"

She shuddered with feeling.

"Every time I think of a white woman in de bush with dat nasty mad negar man, I lose my appetite. Now it give me a headache on top of everything else. Where you put the aspirin?"

Busha told her.

"What is de world coming to, Oh Lord?" she invoked wearily on her way to the medicine cabinet.

Aloysius was depressed afterwards with Inga. It took two strong doses of pum-pum to make him feel better. But even then he still complained about the way she had carried on before Busha.

"All right. All right," Inga snapped. "Forget him. He is of no importance."

"Busha no trouble you. You go on too bad with him, man. Is not right. Busha come see me, no you."

"Vhat he vant, anyhow?"

Aloysius chuckled.

"Dey want me to bowl in de cricket match 'gainst Walker's Wood."

"Cricket match? You play cricket vith him?"

"De big match. Everybody in de village who can play want play. Walker's Wood must beat dis time. Must!"

The woman was pensive. The open fire flared and crackled and lit up her white face with a sinister roseate glow.

"I think I know vhat is wrong with this island," she said softly.

"Vhat's wrong?"

"Too many lies. Not enough hate."

"Vhat dat?"

"There is reason for hate. Poor people everywhere you look. A few rich people. There should be hate. But there is no hate. That is vhat wrong with this place. It needs more hate."

"Hate?"

"In Europe, ve have lots of hate. This is why Europe is strong and rich. This is vhy Jamaica is poor."

"Bumbo," whispered the tree. "Listen dis now."

Chapter Fourteen

Inga and Aloysius went for many walks throughout the surrounding countryside in the days that followed. Sometimes they trekked over empty pastures where only cows and goats looked up lazily as they tramped past, and sometimes they took side roads travelled by hagglers and cultivators and schoolchildren who lived in nearby mountain villages. Old people would pass them on the road and exchange formal, polite greetings in voices that dripped with caution and questioning. Passing schoolchildren would wait until the pair were safely in the distance and then scream out, "Mad-man and white woman!" and fly with terrified squeals into the bushland. Rotund country matrons, their bellies girthed with aprons, peered suspiciously out of their doorways when these two walked past. Even the birds seemed to Aloysius to turn and gawk at this sight of the mad and the white keeping company.

So they walked every day in the early afternoons, in the mornings, sometimes with the blush of the setting sun on the rolling pastures and the long still shadows of the evening melting in the blur of twilight all around them.

One day on just such a walk Inga found and took a second lover. It did not matter that Aloysius threw tantrums and shed tears and begged her to be faithful to him and howled oaths and blasphemies. One hood would not do her, she said stonily. She needed at least two.

So she invited a young butcher, a man who went by the name of Service, into the camp and gave him a grind in the dirt.

They met this butcher one afternoon. They were tramping on the asphalt road on the way to the seacoast when they spotted a young man who was preparing to butcher a goat.

"Let's vatch," Inga said.

They sat on a grey cut-stone wall and watched.

The goat was tied to a tree and bleating like a child while the young man sat on a rock and sharpened his knife. He did not know that he was being watched. All he knew was that he liked his knife to be sharp enough to etch a thin red line across a swollen throat. He worked on the blade with the humourless vanity that workmen take in their tools.

The goat cried hoarsely, rolled its eyes, and strained at the rope around its neck. The wind soughed across the pastures and the bushes and trees trembled as though it told a fearsome story.

Finished with the knife, the young man grabbed the goat by the legs and wrestled it down on its side. He bound its forelegs and hindlegs with twine. Still whistling softly, monotonously through his teeth, he tied a rope to the bound hind legs of the goat and hoisted the struggling animal upside down from the limb of a tree.

The goat screamed – a falsetto wail filled with terror and helplessness. It fought vainly against the rope; it jerked and danced on its end like a hanged man. The young man chuckled at its antics.

He showed the goat the knife, holding it up so the animal could see its silver grin, resting the icy flat side of the blade against its throat. The goat shuddered and shrank from the chill of the blade, wailing in the shrill voice of a terrified virgin. Wrapping his thick, muscular arms around the goat's neck, the young man carefully palpated the big artery that snaked up the side of its neck.

One deft flick of his wrist and he had sliced open the soft throat. The wound gaped as vulgar and gaudy as the painted red mouth on a whore. Blood sheeted out of the slit throat and rained onto the earth. The goat exploded into a twitching spasm of death.

Then the animal was swinging lifeless from the limb, the soughing breeze licking at a tangle of blue veins and white bone bared in its throat.

Whistling silently between his teeth, the young man stepped back and surveyed his handiwork.

He placed an enamel basin under the hanging goat, punctured its swollen abdomen, and unzipped the belly with one smooth slice. The intestines slithered out of the body like an engorged snake suddenly freed from its feasting in a dark place.

He stuck the knife inside the belly of the goat and pared off whole bloody organs that splattered into the basin like overripe fruit.

He began skinning the goat. He cut open the forelegs, and he peeled back the skin, carefully exposing the striations of the muscles enamelled over bone, the formal purple lines of embedded arteries and veins, the sinews running like streaks of rich ore in the dark mines of the flesh.

The skinned goat glistened like a new-born infant. It swung in the breeze as the young man worked, whistling his tuneless song between his teeth. He laid out the skin on the ground, turning the side pasted with thick blood towards the sun.

So the young man worked on the goat, sawing off its head and placing it on a rock where it stared with grim fixity at the surrounding grasslands and hills like the statue of an eminent dwarf; so he hacked and chopped, extracting roasts and ribs and loins from the carcass, which he arranged in a neat pile in the enamel basin. And when he was done, he placed the head of the goat – its eyes wide open – on top of the rubble of bone and meat.

"He is an artist," Inga breathed.

"Him a butcher," Aloysius muttered. "Vhat artist?"

She scaled the wall and headed down the slope towards the young man and the dead goat.

"You don't even know butcher from artist," Aloysius carped, following after her with a mounting sense of foreboding.

Inga aimed the camera at the dead goat, stalking around it like a hunter, taking pictures at every angle. Aloysius shrank back and would not meet the piercing stare of the decapitated head mounted on the ruins of bone and flesh.

"You know vhat you are," Inga said breathlessly to the young man, her eyes shining with discovery. "You are a sculptor. An artist."

The young man beamed.

"I do not tell a joke," she said. "This is a Picasso. This is how a goat looks to an artist."

"Come here, man," the goat head said to Aloysius.

Aloysius shrank behind a bush.

"Vhat is your name?" Inga asked the young man. "Mine is Inga."

"Me name Service," the young man grunted.

"Service? Is that your given name?"

"Dat's me first name. Me modder name Johnson."

"I vill call this picture, 'hieroglyphic goat'," Inga said, taking another shot of the pile of bone and flesh in the basin. "This one vill vin a prize."

"What dat she call me?" the goat head asked Aloysius.

"Bumbo," Aloysius whispered, shielding his eyes.

"This is the first time in my life I have truly seen a goat," Inga gushed. "It is a vork of art."

"Oh de!" a voice bellowed from the top of a nearby hill. "What madman and white woman doing 'pon me land?"

They turned and saw a portly cultivator who had hired the young man to butcher the goat trundling down the hillside determinedly towards them.

So now there were three of them in the bush, and it did not matter that Aloysius wept and the tree shrieked that it could not stand to have two men grinding one woman right under its nose or that even the nearby bushes scolded the lewdness of this living arrangement, still there were now three of them in the bush: Aloysius, the German woman, and this butcher named Service.

Service showed up at the camp because Inga had invited him and had even drawn him a map showing where she and Aloysius lived in the bush; and when he came two nights later he brought with him a chunk of meat he'd stolen from his latest butchering job and sat around the fire while Aloysius baked the meat with wild pepper and thyme in a hole dug in the ground and filled with charcoal.

Occasionally Service would lift his head and peer wonderingly through the flickering glare of the fire from Aloysius to the white woman. But most of the time he listened and nodded and watched Inga with a hungry look.

Aloysius cooked the meat in sullen silence. After a few minutes of aimless talking, Inga stood up and signalled with her eyes for Service to follow her. He stood up, touched the knife in his belt, flicked a wary glance at Aloysius, then disappeared with her into the dark mouth of the night.

Aloysius collapsed against the flame heart tree.

"She giving 'way me pum-pum," he sobbed faintly to the tree.

"Giving it 'way like grieving eye drop water," the tree grunted.

"Why she do dis to me, eh? What me do her?"

"Who can understand woman? Never mind, Aloysius. If me had pum-pum, me would save it all for you."

"Thank you," Aloysius mumbled.

"Me would put it inna shoe box and take it out only when you want a piece."

"Thank you."

"Me would hire blue stripe constable fe guard it from hood."

"All right."

"Me would put it inna refrigerator like you supposed to do wid dead fish."

"All right. All right."

"Me would put one bad dog in me drawers and tie him up next to me pum-pum bush to bite any hood that try sneak a grind."

"Hush up! Me heart broke. You make it worse."

"Don't me tell you not to bring dat rass woman inna de bush?" the tree said spitefully. "Don't me tell you so? Don't me beg you fe leave rass woman where you find her?"

"Every man make mistake."

"Mistake, you bumbo! You bring de rass woman here in de bush where we used to live peaceful. You grind her right before me eye. You make her wee-wee 'pon me root and bite me trunk. Den you talk 'bout mistake because she give 'way de pum-pum to butcher man."

Aloysius could only sit by the fire, peer into the darkness where they had disappeared, and lick his wounded pride like a beaten dog.

But this first grind went badly. The butcher hurried the business and finished too soon, and Inga got vexed and boxed him on the ear. He flew into a rage and reached for his knife, which she wrestled away from him and flung into the dark grassland.

The two of them returned to the fire scowling and snarling at each other.

"Why you lick me for?" Service screamed indignantly.

"Because you go too fast!" Inga hissed.

"You thump up me side! You broke me rib!"

He peeled up his shirt and fingered an ugly welt against his ribcage.

"Look what dis damn white woman do to me side, sah?" Service whined to Aloysius in a voice suddenly thick with petulance and fear. "She thump up me side when me not looking."

"Is all right," Aloysius bent and squinted carefully at the welt. "Me'll wee-wee 'pon it for you and it'll get better."

"Wee-wee? You mad rass, you! Wee-wee 'pon who? Who you goin' wee-wee on?"

"Me just trying fe help you!"

"Help me by wee-weeing on me? You think me is a chamber pot?"

"Next time you pull a knife on me," Inga growled, "this is vhat I do to you."

She hammered a scruffy bush with the violent and athletic kick of a Chinaman in a kung-fu movie.

"Extreme Unchion!" the bush howled. "Call de priest! Me need Extreme Unchion!"

"Inga!" Aloysius cried. "De bush no trouble you! Him is a Catholic bush!"

"Extreme Unchion!" the bush bawled. "Me need last rites! Almighty God, me soul goin' a purgatory! 'Someday! Someday!' Dat how de clock tick in Purgatory! 'Someday! Someday!' Now me goin' dere just like de nun dem warn me!"

"Hush up!" Aloysius snapped.

"Who you telling hush up?" Service snarled.

"No you, man!" Aloysius said hastily. "Me mean de bush."

"Me shouldna listen to de nun dem!" the bush howled.

Inga sat down and spat at the fire. Her mouth-water made a sizzling sound as it bounced off a hot rock. Service slunk into the night.

She opened up her book and began to write about her experiences of the evening. Aloysius sat down limply beside her and broke into a sorrowful sobbing.

"You give 'way me pum-pum," he sobbed.

"Vhat?"

He was convulsed with tears. He could not help himself.

"You give 'way me pum-pum! You give it 'way right under me nose! Right before me eye, you give 'way me pum-pum."

"One man is not sufficient for me. I am a voman vith a large sexual appetite. I need two men, three men. I tell you that already."

"You break me heart. Vhy you must break me heart so?"

He was sobbing hysterically. Inga put down her book and looked searchingly at him.

"Look," she said impatiently, "you are wrong. I did not give it away as you said. It is still here. I show you."

She got up and wriggled out of her pants and stood before him naked from the waist down.

"See?"

Aloysius looked up and shrieked.

"It gone!" he wailed. "The butcher thief it! No more pum-pum!"

"Idiot! It is not gone. Here. Touch me here!"

He did and gave off a ravenous howl.

"All dat left is a smooth and round spot like bald head parson! No more pum-pum! Pum-pum gone forever!"

He was so hysterical that Inga wrestled him to the ground and pinned him there while he wriggled and shrieked incoherently. She slapped him hard across the face and shook him like a child.

"Listen to me, you fool! Jealousy has made you blind. Look at me! Look!"

Sniffing and blinking through his tears, Aloysius looked.

"It no gone?" he whimpered.

"Of course not. Vhere can it go?"

"But when me just look little while ago, all me see was one bald spot."

"The light is bad. Here, touch me."

"Me can't see it, either," the tree cried. "Make me touch it, too."

"Make me get up," Aloysius said, sniffling.

She released him.

He stood up and shook his head vigorously as though he were trying to rouse himself from drowsiness.

"You bring vater to me eye, Inga. Vhen me live here alone vith just me and de tree, de only time vater ever come to me eye is vhen me lonely. Now you stay here vith me and cause me grief and bring vater to my eye."

"If I tell you one time I tell you a hundred time not to bring dat woman inna de bush," the tree scolded.

A twig popped like a bone in the night. They turned and saw Service lurking on the edge of the glow from the fire.

"You didn't have to lick me so hard, man," he mumbled with a downcast look.

Still naked from the waist down, Inga looked from the one black man to the other.

She stood up: a hundred red tongues of fire licked at the whiteness of her thick body unsheathed in its nakedness from the waist down. The eyes of the two black men darted like moths around the pum-pum.

She settled on her haunches and began to do long division in the dirt – the arithmetic problem that in the exercise books of children always takes on the shape of the mouse. The answer unravelled into the familiar tail that got smaller and smaller until it trickled down to a remainder.

"Let me make one thing clear," she said, standing up. "I am the boss. You understand? Otherwise this cannot be. You understand?"

"Vhy must one person be boss, Inga?" Aloysius asked, preparing barrister arguments.

"Because only one person has the pum-pum," she said.

The butcher nodded solemnly and sat before the fire.

"Pum-pum rule," he intoned.

Aloysius stabbed at the dirt with his toe.

"Pum-pum hold portfolio over dis jurisdiction," he muttered.

"From Socialism to Capitalism to Pum-pumism," a bush screeched. "Lawd Jesus God, what now on de head of poor Jamaica?"

Chapter Fifteen

Under the rule of pum-pum there were civic improvements made in the plot of pastureland in the bush: a house was built. It was a house such as poor men have made in Jamaica since the malarial beginnings of the Fallen Empire. Its walls were made of wattled sticks, sealed with river mud, and stank like the dried hide of an old animal. It had a sloping roof of plywood covered with galvanized zinc sheets and a dirt floor overlaid with sheets of cardboard.

On the day the house was finished Inga took numerous pictures of it and made endless drawings and notes. It was her idea to build the house. She had given Aloysius and Service the money to buy the few materials needed and told them where she wanted it raised under the sheltering overhand of the flame heart tree.

By the time the rainy season began the three of them were living in the house in these the days when rain roared on the roof and the nights when the pasture blew with the chill of an ocean breeze.

"Dey build chicken coop house," Busha reported to his meeting of the cricket club. "Now dere's three of dem in it."

"Three of dem?" the parson asked incredulously.

"Three of dem," Busha said. "Two man and dat woman."

The parson looked at the doctor, who looked at the inspector, who looked at Busha, who shook his head with foreboding.

The four of them silently brooded on the algebra of two men with one woman.

"Dis is a case for hellfire if ever dere was one," mumbled the parson.

"Damn foolishness," the doctor snapped.

"Where Sarah?" the inspector asked wistfully. "Butchering more chicken?"

"She have a running stomach," Busha chuckled. "Morning, noon and night she sit on the toilet. Just like she find a new throne."

During the month that followed it rained nearly every afternoon, with the sound of knuckles pounding on the zinc roof of the small house. Then the skies cleared and a crisp evening breeze rose up off the mountains and the land glimmered in the sunset and gave off the fresh smell of the infant earth.

At night the darkness blew gently into the valley on a cool breeze. In the mornings a thick fog steeped the green loveliness of the land in a hushed pool of whiteness.

"This is the way the vorld used to be," Inga declared one morning as she stepped out of the small house and sniffed at the fog. "It reminds me of the days vhen I vas a cow."

"A cow? What you talking about?" Aloysius was scratching himself all over as he did every morning.

"In another life I vas a cow."

"How you know dat?"

"I vas a very good milker, too. The man who owned me always told me that."

"How much milk you give?" Aloysius asked.

Yawning loudly, Service shambled out of the house.

"You build the fire," Inga told him.

"Me build it yesterday."

"Build it again," she said. "Aloysius, you go draw the vater."

"Why always me drawing de vater?"

"Because I say that is vhat you must do. Now do it vhile I take a valk."

She wandered off into the thick fog and disappeared into the cloying whiteness.

"How you know you vas a cow?" Aloysius called after her.

"What you talking about, you mad brute?" Service grunted.

"She say she used to be a cow."

"Me making new rule," Service growled, stooping down to arrange the wood for the fire. "No more butter bun for me. You go second from now on. You take butter bun."

"Dat is not my decision," Aloysius said with dignity.

"Well, me make de decision now. New rule. No more butter bun for me. Learn dat now. Madman don't know de difference between butter bun and dry bun. A-hoa."

"You don't hold authority over dat business," Aloysius said boldly.

"Hold you rass!" Service faced him threateningly. "Who you talking to?"

Inga materialized out of the fog.

"Aloysius," she said impatiently, "go for vater."

"How much milk you give? I vas vaiting to hear de answer."

She screwed up her face and looked intently at the ground.

"Me make new rule," Service scowled. "Him not goin' tell you 'bout it so me goin' tell you meself. No more butter bun for dis man. You hear me? No more butter bun!"

"Vhat you talking about?" she snapped.

"Why me must go second last night? Why me get de butter bun? Why me no go first?"

"You don't like it, you get out of here. Now shut up, I'm thinking."

"But why me go second three time in a row? Dat not fair."

"Thirty gallons. One morning I gave thirty gallons of milk."

Aloysius whistled appreciatively.

"Thirty gallon! Dat a whole heap o' milk."

"Three time in a row me get butter bun. Fair is fair, man. Three time in a row. What kind of business is dis? One man get butter bun three times in a row."

"The farmer say to me, 'I vish I had a hundred cows like you. I vould be a rich man.' You know vhat I say to him?"

"Vhat?"

"Mooo!"

Aloysius and Inga laughed loudly like schoolchildren.

She stopped laughing and gave the stooping Service a quick kick in the bottom.

"Dat's what me get in dis place," he muttered sullenly. "Butter bun and batty kick. Dat's all me good for."

"Look, you idiot!" she cuffed him hard on the side of the head. "Better butter bun than no bun at all."

"True," Aloysius agreed quickly. "Me remember days around here when me didn't even have …"

"Hush you rass mouth!" Service hissed at him. "Me don't want to hear nothing from you!"

"Vill you go and draw the vater!" Inga snapped, her mood turning ugly.

"Me going! Me going!" Aloysius protested.

He hoisted the kerosene can on top of his head and set off whistling into the fog.

Every day Service left early in the morning to seek butchering jobs. He returned late in the evenings when the shadows of the trees were lean and bony fingers clawing at the grasslands. Sometimes he brought with him a piece of meat or pork and sometimes a live chicken. He would cut off its head with a sharp whack of the machete and sit and watch the headless chicken flutter blindly across the yard, blood pumping out of the neck stump. He liked to kneel and peer at the severed head lying in the dirt, the beak sucking vainly for air, the upright eye lidding over with a thick cream.

Aloysius could not bear to witness this useless suffering and would quickly leave. He would hurry away into the bushland and sit down under a naseberry tree and caulk up his ears with his fingers so as not to listen to the thunk of the machete as it bit into neck bone.

"Another chicken kill, eh?" the naseberry tree remarked one evening.

"Him love death too much," Aloysius grumbled.

It was in the eyes of this butcher that Aloysius saw love of death – the black eyes that tunnelled, like two worm holes, into a dark place. When Service was not watching Inga hungrily out of the corner of his eyes, when he was not poring over the machete or the sharp knife, his eyes would fix themselves on a distant spot and gaze at something he alone could see.

"He vas a beaten child," Inga said to Aloysius one day.

"How you know dat?" Aloysius asked.

"I know. I can tell."

"Who beat him?"

"Someone big and cruel."

"You don't know dat."

"I know," Inga said airily.

"Vhat about me? Anybody beat me?" Aloysius asked.

"Yes."

"Hah! Who beat me?"

"God. He is the one who beat you."

"Vhat you talking about? I never see God in me life!"

But she refused to continue with this line of argument, which made Aloysius vexed, so vexed that he sat that evening beside the butcher and recounted the conversation to him in order to get someone to laugh with him at how foolish the German was in her speculations.

But the butcher merely looked stonily at Aloysius and would not talk about his past or argue about the German's speculations or even chuckle at the wild notion that Aloysius had been beaten by the Almighty.

And he was the sort of man – this silent butcher – whom you could not press too hard because of what you saw coiled deep in the well-bottom of his eyes, watching you.

One week in this rainy season Inga decided that for the time being she had had enough to do with hood. She decided that it was a time for breezing out her body.

Breezing meant that she walked around the camp naked when the breeze blew, that sometimes she lay flat on her back in the guinea grass and hoisted up the pum-pum to the sky to air it out. This was the season when the breeze came off the slopes of the mountain smelling pungently of burning wood, when the trees shook to its touch and the grassland rippled with catspaws.

During this week of breezing even the sight of a hood threw her into a violent temper and made her chop viciously with kung-fu motions. So Aloysius and Service walked around the small house with their manhoods flowering in their pants and did their best not to look at her as she sprawled out on the grassland with her eyes closed and the breeze cooling her nakedness.

Service killed two chickens in the breezing week and gnashed his teeth and one night even bawled out loud for someone from his past. Aloysius wandered in and out of the camp holding vehement discussions with bushes and squabbling endlessly with the flame heart tree. One night he sat outside the small house and recited every one of his thousand names.

But soon the breezing days were over and she came to her senses and once more demanded hood from them. Once agan they were able to do up their flies without fear of snagging their manhoods between the sharp teeth of a zipper.

"De breezing nearly kill me," Aloysius whispered one morning to the flame heart tree. "One more week o' de breezing and me dead."

"You can't make pum-pum rule you so," the tree scolded.

"Dis is de portfolio of pum-pum," Aloysius said helplessly.

"Pum-pum don't rule over me."

"Well, anyhow, everything air out good now so I suppose breezing time over and done wid."

"Me always thought pum-pum did air condition," the tree said.

"No, man," chuckled Aloysius with a hard-won knowledge. "Pum-pum must air out and draw fresh breath once in a while. Dat's why church woman is so miserable, 'cause dey force deir pum-pum to live inna dark place and draw stale breath like worm. When what pum-pum need is good breezing."

"Is true, you know!"

"But is de parson dem fault, for dey is de one dat preach dat pum-pum must lurk inna crotch like rat in a tree!"

"Must tie up like bad dog!"

"Eh ah! And why? Who pum-pum ever bite?'

"Who, indeed? Since when pum-pum have teeth?"

The villagers did not take well to this scandalous sight of a white woman and two black men keeping house in the bush. Tongues wagged morning, noon and night over this arrangement and wherever Aloysius, Service and Inga walked together in the village they were met with fish-eyed stares from windows, shops, and verandas. When they had passed, heads would shake with foreboding and mouths would whisper out of their corners and knowing smiles would crack lewdly after them.

Old women, remembering the White Witch of Rose Hall who had enticed young slave men into her bed and murdered them when she had wearied of their bodies, thought Inga a witch and openly said so. Slack young girls rudely boasted that it was the sweetness of black hood that made the white woman keep two men, and when they passed Inga in the streets they called to her impertinently as thought they knew her deepest secrets.

Inga was impervious to insult, to innuendo, to wagging heads or lewd smiles. She swaggered through the village with the cocksure step of one who had lived there all her life. She tramped into dirty shops that stank of fetid cheese and saltfish brine and she plopped down her elbows on the grimy counters and ordered what she wanted as though no eyes were peering sharply at her from every corner, as though voices had not hushed at her appearance and backs had not stiffened and mouths had not snaked into grim lines.

Many a morning she passed in the cemetery behind Mr. Shubert's small shop, sitting against the trunk of a gnarled lignum vitae tree, a pad open on her knees, making a sketch of the weathered tombstones that rose crookedly out of the green earth like bad teeth.

"Is me family she drawing, you know," Busha said with alarm when he heard of the German's practice from Mr. Shubert.

"But me Mumma is dere too, Busha," Mr. Shubert reminded him.

"I know dat," Busha snapped. "But for every one Shubert in dat graveyard you goin' find ten McIntoshes."

Mr. Shubert shrugged.

"What de rass is dis woman doing, drawing me family for?" Busha ranted. "Damn out of order, man! Dis Jamaica is de only country in de world where even when a man dead and in him grave him must still pose for tourists."

Now in the countryside of every parish are wicked young schoolboys who act as though Almighty God had appointed them watchmen and criers of the defects, traits, and infirmities possessed by otherwise decent people. If a man has an ear missing because of a horrible accident, the boys will shriek out "One Ear Hole" when he passed them on the street. If a woman has a big batty they will trumpet, "Big Batty Woman!" as she flounces past.

Grim silence is the only defence against these taunting urchins. Violence does no good because they repay it in kind and with banker's interest. Argument does no good because they are schooled in the urchin art of screeching out graphic nastiness about bowel movements and private parts. Chasing them does no good because they fly headlong into the bush flinging taunts over their shoulders.

So the only thing a big batty woman can do is to hold her head high and act as though she does not have a big batty and that the urchins are quite mistaken in shrieking so. Often this attempt at aloofness will drive these wicked boys to bellow their observations at a terrifying volume so that the poor woman's progress is winded to everyone ahead as the approach of a big batty, not a woman in her Sunday clothes on her way to bow her knee to the Almighty, but a big batty with legs and arms and a mouth and two eyes, a big batty that has boastfully put on a calico frock, a veiled hat, and high-heeled shoes and taken to the streets putting on airs like a bogus voter.

These urchins began shouting too at Inga.

At first she did not understand the boys and mistakenly thought they were greeting her in a boisterously good-humoured way. Once she even shouted back playfully at them.

But then one day as she was walking to the strip of pasture where Service did his butchering they blasted in her ear "Two Hood Woman" so loud that she flinched.

It was a Saturday evening, villagers were streaming past on their way from the market, and the urchins were perched on a stretch of broken wall beside the road.

When she realized what the boys had said, Inga roared with anger and chased after them. They piled off the wall and scattered into the bushland shrieking, "Two Hood Woman! Two Hood Woman!"

She scaled the wall and singled one out and ran him down in the middle of the cow pasture.

Astonished villagers stood stock still on the roadway and watched.

The boy threw a wild thump at her and was felled on the grass by a wicked clout to the side of his head.

She started tearing off his clothes. He screamed and wriggled and kicked at her, his voice echoing across the pasture to the foot of the mountains, scattering flocks of goats and herds of cows.

Amazed, the villagers watched from the wall as she ripped off the boy's clothes. Then she began to take off her own clothes, at which the naked boy scrambled to his feet and tore across the pasture with the white woman in furious pursuit.

The torn shirt flapping off his back, the nude boy dodged and darted with the German hard on his heels, and he bawled out in a terrifying voice for his Puppa and Mumma.

"Me God!" one villager whispered to another.

With a horrible scream, the boy vanished into the thicket with the white woman close behind him.

Some villagers jumped the wall and rushed into the bush to see the outcome of the chase. The rest stood in the road and loudly debated what they had just witnessed. A crowd gathered and awaited the outcome from those who had followed the white woman and the naked boy.

They returned a few minutes later, blowing hard and waving their hands.

"Dem gone."

"Gone where?"

"Gone up de road. Gone a bush."

"Why she tear off her clothes so?"

"Me no know! Me never see nothing like dis in all me born days!"

"Me know why she do it."

"Why?"

"To rum her batty in de boy face."

"But kiss me neck!"

"Sweet Jesus, listen to dis now!"

"Is batty rub she goin' give him. Serve him right. Dem nasty boy always troubling people."

"Is not batty rub him goin' get! Is grind she goin' grind him!"

"Foolishness! What kind a thing is dat? A boy call a woman a nasty name and she hold him down and give him grind? What kind of sense dat make?"

"Me say, is grind she goin' grind him! Me hear 'bout dis woman from long time. Is a hard woman dis, you know!"

"Me say, batty rub!"

"Grind!"

"Batty rub!"

"Grind!"

"Batty rub, you damn fool! You think woman give out grind like dat!"

"Grind, you ugly monkey you! She goin' grind him till him neck broke. You didn't know pum-pum kill man worse dan gunshot?"

"What you think, Missah Williams?" someone asked an old black man who stood on the edge of the crowd leaning heavily on his cane.

Missah Williams didn't know. He had never heard of batty rub before. He never knew that women held down men and gave them a grind. All this was new to him.

The crowd was convulsed. Missah Williams did not know whether to join in the general merriment or look vexed at this mocking of one of his age.

The people gathered their baskets, live chickens and ground provisions and started trekking up the road that climbed the face of the mountain in switchbacks and led to the distant villages.

One rude girl walked beside Missah Williams, teasing him and putting slack questions to him.

"Eighty-eight years now I live on dis earth, you know," Missah Williams said in a feeble but proud voice. "Every Sunday I go to church and thank God for long life."

"A lie, Missah Williams!" The girl rolled her eyes saucily at him. "Is woman you go look."

"Woman?" Mr. Williams stopped in his tracks and stared at her with alarm. "What would I do with woman? At my age woman would kill me stone dead."

"No, Missah Williams, no say dat. Dat thing prolong life, make white hair turn black again. It make teeth grow back and kinky hair turn straight."

"Me never knew it was medicine," Mr. Williams mumbled. "Dis is de new Jamaica way of thinking. In my day we was only trying to have children."

One afternoon the people of the boy Inga had chased showed up at the house and there was a good deal of shrieking of threats back and forth. The boy's mother clutched a vicious rockstone and took on oath that she would kill a white woman with it before the sun set. The father stood behind the mother, carried a big stick, and muttered that he was looking for a blonde head to crack. An uncle or two and a cousin sheltered with him in the shadow of the stout mother. Service sat on the dirt holding a machete in one hand and a knife in the other and raked the group with a murderous stare. Aloysius ran from one to the other trying to calm everyone down.

At first Inga paid no attention to them but soon she was drawn into the quarrel and started yelling back insults.

The mother bellowed out her grievances on top of her voice.

"She chase me pickney inna de bush! She chase me one boy child like him is goat inna de bush! She rip off de very clothes on him back and make him walk de street naked! She hold him down and do something to de boy so wicked and nasty dat to dis day him won't tell me what she do!"

"He called me a name!" Inga replied.

"Name?" the mother shrieked indignantly. "Him call you name? I goin' kill you bumbo! Is only name him call you? Is you bumbo I goin' kill!?"

"You vant to fight?" Inga invited. "Come. I fight you now. I fight you right here."

"Fight?" the father scoffed. "Me wife don't fight nobody, you know! When my wife fight is murder she committing. A-hoa!"

"Hush up you mouth!" the woman flung at him over her shoulder. "Make me talk!"

"No fighting!" Aloysius begged. "No fighting. Ve not fighting today."

"Me say she hold down me pickney, you know Missah Aloysius?" the woman appealed to him. "She strip de clothes off him back. Is naked him come home naked, you know?"

And so it went on for an hour or two, the quarrel pulsating between nastiness, rancor and grumbling. Eventually, the screeching family members beat a sullen retreat, trailing violent oaths and blasphemous threats after them. They vanished to a hill where they made a last stand, discharging volleys of bad words. Aloysius raced between the house and the withdrawing family, trying to patch matters up and occasionally igniting them to another blast of furious cursing.

"I don't understand these people," Inga muttered. "They come here to make a lot of noise."

"Dey need chopping," Service said darkly.

Blowing hard from running, Aloysius returned to the house.

"Dem gone!" he panted. "Me quiet dem down. What a worries 'pon me head today. Lawd Jesus, Inga, what you do to dem pickney?"

She grinned wickedly and would not tell.

After that incident the boys never again called out their mockeries to Inga. They sat on the same stretch of wall and they shouted their biting epithets at everyone who passed. But they did not shout at Inga.

On a Saturday morning they sat on the wall and chorused out loud greetings to "One Nose Hole," "Cave In Batty," "Crook Foot," and "Peel Head Parson." Even when Busha drove past the boys screeched out, "Big Belly Busha!" after him.

But only stony silence greeted Inga. She walked past the wall slowly, even pausing to look hard at the urchins and pretending to sniff a wild orchid that grew on the shoulder of the road.

When she finally moved away it was with the hesitant step of the day-dreamer.

"Fatty Chin!" she heard them yell.

Inga turned and saw an old woman wobbling past the taunting boys, a heavy basket on her head, an ugly chin dripping off her face, an aura of grim dignity in her every leaden step.

Days later Inga said to Aloysius, "I am the only one vithout a name to those boys. I am sorry I did vhat I did. Now I feel lonely and unnamed."

"You can take one o' me name," Aloysius said. "Me have a thousand o' dem."

"Vhich one can I have?"

" 'Impracticable.' Take dat one."

"I don't like it."

"You want 'Loquacious'?"

"That is not a voman's name."

"Take one of him name!" Service spat with disgust. "Which one o' dem madder, to rass?"

So it went in the first weeks under the rule of pum-pum.

Chapter Sixteen

Busha took sick one night in this same month, awaking with a crushing pain in his chest. At first he lay quietly in his bed hoping the pain would go away, but when it did not he got up and padded to a window and peered out the burglar bars at the dark pastures.

A night bird sang and the fields shone with the crystalline blue light of a half moon.

Why me? Busha asked himself peevishly. Why did he have to be the one to wake up with a pain in his chest when so many other hearts beat soundly in this district? With almost no effort at all he could count scores of peaceful sleepers within a walking distance of where he now stood worrying over the pain in his chest. Just to prove it he began a head count of the sleepers in the district. Down the road slept Mrs. Thompson and her seven children; over that dark ridge were the Lydfords, all fifteen of them no doubt snoring; up the hill a piece were the Crockers, who numbered eight slumbering children, one husband, one wife, the wife's mother, and ten dogs.

All this fretful thinking and nighttime arithmetic made the pain worse. Busha gritted his teeth and tried to ignore it.

But there was no ignoring such pain. It came from too deep down inside his chest; it caused his chest to ache like a bad tooth. Busha peered over his shoulder at the bed where Sarah lay sleeping.

"Everybody sleeping peacefully," he said loudly in the dark room.

Sarah did not stir so Busha bellowed:

"De whole world sleeping!"

Sarah bolted upright in bed.

"Hubert! Hubert, is dat you?"

"Me one."

"What you doing by de window? Why you bawling out on top o' your voice for?"

"I have pain in me chest."

Sarah jumped out of bed with alarm and to his side.

"You think you having a heart attack?"

"I don't know what I having. I just feel bad."

"Oh, my God, Hubert! I should drive you to de hospital!"

She dressed hurriedly and helped Busha into his field clothes. Then they set out in the dark night for the hospital, which lay some thirty miles away on the seacoast down a narrow road that wound over mountains, slumbering villages, and darkened fields.

"Whatever happen to me, Sarah," Busha pleaded as the car's headlights splashed on the tombstones of the village graveyard, "don't bury me in dat place. I beg you don't put me where donkey and cow and goat goin' trample on me grave!"

"Hubert, don't say dat!" Sarah scolded. "You goin' make me have an accident."

Every event, every incident in Busha's life had occurred in this parish, near this same road over which the car now careened. Landmarks flashed past in the darkness, evoking memory and gloomy commentary out of him.

"To think I might dead in Walker's Wood," Busha moaned as they drove through the shuttered village of that name, "Lawd God, don't make me dead in Walker's Wood! Anywhere else but this place. We supposed to play dem cricket next month."

"Don't talk like dat!" Sarah snapped, nearly ramming a roadside wall.

"Right in dis spot I used to shoot bird with me Daddy," Busha mumbled later on, "now I come to dead in it."

"Hubert!"

Then later:

"Remember de night we catch crab here, Sarah? You catch crab in a place one night and de next thing you know you dead in dat same place. Just like a crab."

"For God's sake, Hubert!" Sarah screeched.

They also passed those places where Busha silently remembered begging a quick nighttime grind from some slack village woman, and he said a quick prayer that he would not die on the spot where he'd committed mortal sin.

Eventually the car headed down the dark throat of Fern Gully where Busha had done nothing of significance except driving through and witness tourists gawking at the clutter of ferns, and he lapsed into gloomily massaging his chest.

Alarmed by his sudden silence, Sarah asked, "Hubert, how you feel?"

Which frightened Busha so much that he snapped, "You testing me to see if I dead? Dat's how to finish off a sick man!"

They screeched into the driveway of the hospital, a scattering of old wooden buildings behind a thick grove of trees with light leaking feebly through an open window, and they tramped down a long, dimly lit breezeway with Busha leaning on Sarah's arm and coughing to attract attention. They hurried past rows and rows of dishevelled beds where patients slept in open wards, and the sweet smell of antiseptic, sickness, and nighttime death assailed Busha's nose and made him wish with all his heart that he had lived a better life.

The matron on duty was catching a doze in a stuffed chair at the end of the dim ward when they found her. Recognizing Busha, she helped him into an examination room where she poked and thumped his chest, looked at his tongue, listened to his heart and pinched his left arm and asked what he's had for supper.

Busha mumbled that in his present condition it was difficult to remember, but he thought he'd had stew peas and green bananas.

"Busha," the matron said, "I think you eat too much dumpling for you dinner."

"What you talking about?" Busha scowled, feeling acutely like he was being taken for a fool. "Dis is Jamaica for you! A man come to de hospital complaining about a pain in him chest and dem tell him him eat too much dumpling. Sarah, carry me outta dis damn place! If I goin' dead tonight make me at least dead in me own bed."

"Dead, Busha?" the matron scoffed. "You can't dead. Who say you can come here and dead on my shift? Come, I going put you inna bed and send for de doctor."

"You think I come all dis way for a joke?" Busha growled. "You think we drive all dese miles because we love night air. Me tell you me chest killing me with pain."

"Busha, I don't hear nothing in de stethoscope. You not flushed. You draw breath freely. You not sweaty."

"How can a man sweat on dis cool night? What's de matter wid you? You a nurse or a obeah woman?"

"Sarah," the matron sighed, "why you don't hush him up for me, eh? Busha, you under my rule now. You goin' do as I say or

I goin' bring out de rod o' correction. Now, you stay here, I goin' get a smock for you and find you a bed."

"Find me a private room," Busha grumbled after her as she disappeared down the hall.

Half an hour later and Busha was tucked into a bed in the far corner of the ward because there were no private rooms available. Sarah stood by his beside and held his hand comfortingly while the matron was rummaging through the supply room for a screen to give him privacy and medicine to help him sleep.

"You damn woman love to stick man wid needle, eh?" Busha quarrelled when the matron returned to give him an injection. "Because God make man to stick woman, you make up you mind you goin' stick him back, eh? No so?"

"What am I goin' do wid him, eh Sarah?" the matron chuckled, shoving the needle deep into his arm.

A few minutes later Busha said a bad word and fell asleep.

Busha woke to hear a sound of death chomping a path towards his bed. Occasionally death would stop and give a weary snort from all the chomping, then it would resume its grim labour. In his drugged state, Busha was having a nightmare about a sermon he had heard a long time ago where the parson had compared death to a goat that eats everything. Death, bellowed the parson, ate man, woman and child just like goat eat guinea grass, tin can, and old shoe. And when it was your time for death to eat you, nothing you did could stop him. Death would chew through a wall to reach you.

So now as Busha awoke from his drugged sleep he heard the sound of death grinding a path to where he slept. He could barely open his eyes because of the influence of the injected medicine, but his heart was racing with the delirious conviction that he had to get up and run before the death goat got near enough to bite.

He moaned, sat up, opened his eyes and looked into the malevolently slanted eyes of a living goat staring at him from four feet away on the veranda.

"RASS!" Busha screamed.

He sprang out of bed, got tangled up in the bedsheets, and toppled against the screen.

The screen clattered to the floor and Busha fell on a fat woman asleep in the next bed.

With a screech of horror, the woman flung him off her bosom. Busha toppled on the floor, rolled under the woman's bed and upset her chamber pot.

A trainee nurse sprinted over to where Busha had fallen and was pinned on all fours under the bed. He kept trying to groggily stand up, each time hoisting the bedspread and mattress and the woman on it violently into the air, drawing horrified shrieks out of her.

"Busha!" the trainee said, getting down on her knees and trying to pull him out from under the bed. "You goin' turn over de bed wid de woman 'pon it."

"De death goat!" Busha raved deliriously.

"Is de watchman goat dat, Busha! Is all right, you know! Is only de watchman goat dat!"

"Him land 'pon top of me and frighten de living daylights outta me!" the fat woman was wailing. "Me think is earthquake and de ceiling drop 'pon me, de weight so sudden and heavy! Lawd God Almighty, de man nearly killed me with fright!"

Busha was led unsteadily back to his bed.

"Out of order!" he mumbled. "Dem have de damn goat dem roaming right up to where people sleeping in de hospital.

Why you don't have cow too and mule and donkey? You might as well if you goin' have goat."

Busha fell back into a drugged sleep. When he awoke again the bed next to him was empty and the floor stank of urine.

An hour later the doctor arrived.

The doctor was a Kingstonian who knew Busha from a long time back. Talking all the while about this year's poor bird season, he listened to Busha's heart thumping through his stethoscope.

"De baldpate flying high, Busha," the doctor complained. "I went out into de bush dis morning and couldn't hit a one. You'd need a rocket to bring one of dem down."

"Why you listening to me back?" Busha asked. "My heart is in de front."

"Draw a breath, Busha," the doctor said. "De whole morning and I see one lapwing."

"Tell me de truth. You think I had a heart attack?"

The doctor said he didn't think so but to be sure he'd do an EKG. He ordered the nurse to bring the EKG machine and she disappeared down the hall and returned rolling a machine to Busha's bedside.

The doctor wired the machine to Busha's chest and turned it on, but it wouldn't work. He fiddled with the knobs on the machine and it still wouldn't come on so he asked the nurse to send and call Hector, who the doctor said was the only one who knew how to get this blasted machine to work right.

From rows and rows of beds in the open ward patients were waking up and peering silently at Busha, who felt stupid and ill-used as though he were the centre of an uncouth scene.

A few minutes later a toothless old black man dressed in ragged khaki pants and a white tee-shirt was standing beside Busha's bed peering at the machine.

"It want a good thump, sah," he told the doctor solemnly. "But is a special spot must thump."

He wriggled between Busha's bed and the machine, studied it for a few seconds, then gave the special spot a solid thump with his right fist. The machine sprang to life and the needles began scrawling across the paper.

"Good God!" Busha muttered. "Is dat what a man heart beat look like? Like chicken scratch a paper."

The doctor chuckled and studied the paper as the machine whirred.

Then he declared in a pompous voice that Busha had definitely not had a heart attack. As bad luck would have it, the matron happened to be passing by Busha's bed just in time to overhear the doctor's diagnosis.

"Is too much dumpling him eat," she gloated. "I tell him so last night, doctor, but him never believe me."

A patient across the hall heard the matron's remark and broke into a chuckle. He muttered something to another patient in the bed beside his and the two of them grinned impertinently at Busha and seemed to be openly gossiping about him.

Feeling profoundly stupid and ridiculed, Busha got out of bed, huddled behind the privacy screen and pulled on his pants.

He was dressed and ready to go when a trainee nurse began stripping the sheets off the bed on which he had fallen in his earlier delirium.

"What happened to de woman who was sleeping dere?" Busha asked.

The trainee looked all around her as though she feared eavesdroppers.

"She gone to meet her Maker, Busha," she whispered, tucking the sheet under the mattress.

"Good God! She dead?"

"This morning. But no because you drop on her, you know, Busha. Her time was overdue. She was supposed to dead from last year."

"Just dead like dat!" Busha marvelled in a awed voice.

"Dese people, Busha, never dead when dem supposed to. Dem dead when dem good and ready, at deir own sweet time."

At the front door the doctor gave Busha a parting shot.

"Busha, is a good thing you leaving us. You killing off all me patients right and left. I don't know what I'm to put on dat poor woman death certificate. 'Falling weight'? 'Heavy load'? 'Sudden burden'?"

The doctor laughed heartily at his own humour.

None of this struck Busha as at all funny. Feeling wounded and humiliated, he left the hospital and drove grimly back up into the mountains with Sarah dozing wearily at his side.

The freshness of morning had not yet burned off the fields as Busha drove upland, and the air still tanged with the coolness of dew. He passed hordes of uniformed schoolchildren on their way to school, workers trekking slowly down to the fields, cattle browsing in cool pastures, and he felt glad to be alive. The road where he had trapped the thief, bought the hog, or even stolen the grind didn't seemed fearful in daylight. It even struck Busha that he would be better dropping dead among the fresh air and lovely scenery of such a stretch of road than dying in the dingy mustiness of a hospital ward. So by the time his car nosed out of Fern Gully, Busha was whistling, occasionally waving to a familiar face he passed on the road, and feeling sorry that this was not Christmas time when he could bawl out greetings of merriness through the car window without seeming peculiar.

Nothing made a man appreciate his life more than a stay in the hospital, Busha was thinking with a shudder. If he had his way he would force all the ungrateful brutes of the world – and God knew that there were millions of them – to overnight in a hospital at least once a month. He would compel whiners to visit a morgue. Chronic complainers he would force to witness an autopsy. (That would shut them up once and for all.)

He was happily scheming up fiendish hospital punishments for malingerers when Sarah stirred, sat up, and looked blearily around at the passing fields.

"Good morning, darling!" Busha said happily.

She raked him with a scowl.

"Dat's all very good for you to say," she grumbled. "You sleep de whole night. I had to sit up in a hard chair. And all because you eat too much blessed dumpling."

She squirmed down in the seat against the door and closed her eyes. Busha lapsed once again into a savage mood.

He was still in this bitter mood when he drove into Montague, turned down the narrow road that snaked through his property, and immediately hallucinated the vision of a stout white woman climbing gingerly into the crown of one of his pear trees.

It took several seconds before his unbelieving brain could register what his eyes had seen. But once the true situation had dawned on him Busha slammed on the brakes of his Land Rover, nearly pitching his sleeping wife into the dashboard, and threw the vehicle into violent reverse.

Then he was out of the Land Rover and yelling on the top of his lungs, "What dat woman doing in me tree? Get out of dat tree!"

Aloysius hurried across the pasture to soothe the wrathful Busha.

"Me tell her not to climb de tree, Busha," he babbled. "But she no listen, sah!"

"Get out of my tree before I call de police and lock you up!" Busha bellowed.

The tree's limbs creaked and bent as Inga began a slow descent.

"You can't come here from Germany and climb people's tree and thief deir fruit!" Busha hollered indignantly. "Dere're laws in dis country. If I catch you on me property again I goin' lock you up! I don't care if you whiter dan Snow White herself! Damn out of order!"

"Imagine," Busha was puffing with rage when he climbed back into the Land Rover, "it's not enough dat dis damn woman seducing half de mad people on de island, now she must come thief from me!"

Nevertheless, catching a praedial thief redhanded in a pear tree was one of the joys of owning property and just what Busha needed to help him forget his humiliations at the hospital. For all his raging, he was feeling better than he had since he'd woken up last night with the pain in his chest.

"But how on earth did dat heavy woman climb way up in dat tree?" Sarah wondered. Craning to look back as Busha roared away, she glimpsed the German standing beside Aloysius and making an obscene gesture after the Land Rover.

From that day on there was open hatred between Busha and Inga.

Chapter Seventeen

Inga was vexed with the world even before Busha had bawled at her for thiefing his pears. Her father had stopped sending money. She'd ignored his order to come home so he'd spitefully cut her purse strings. Everything about Jamaica now struck her as lean and bony: the children looked underfed, the adults hardened and quarrelsome, the scenery a smear of blurry green littered with ramshackle dwellings.

In the days when the money used to flow Inga would get a letter from her father at least every other week. She would read the German handwritten script aloud in a gruff male voice that sounded to Aloysius like the snarling of a cross dog. But even if the letter was cross there would still be big green bills rolled up in its belly.

Then the latest letter came. When she read it aloud the German words exploded juicily inside her mouth; bubbles of spit flew through the air and popped on the grass.

She threw the letter on the ground and lit up her last joint of Sinsemilla.

"What you Daddy say?" Aloysius asked.

"He say come home. No more money."

She picked up the letter and read it again.

"Come home, he says," she repeated.

There was no money in this letter.

One dark country night Inga, Aloysius and Service sat around a fire talking. The fire had gnawed a ragged hole out of the darkness and the three of them were huddled inside it, their faces tinted red from the glare of the flames. They were ruminating about moonlight foolishness, swapping thoughts about everything from why Japanese men loved to eat so much mushroom to why woman had a fatter batty than man. Everything that Inga said Service would contradict. She would tell him to shut up and he would either growl and snarl or whimper about how she was cruel to him. But when the conversation moved off to another topic, he would enrage her again with more contradicting opinion.

Just the week before he had annoyed Inga so much that she had stopped giving him pum-pum altogether, reducing him to endless whining about how it was wicked for a white woman to treat a negar man so. Whenever he was vexed with Inga he called her a white woman. This name would goad her into a nasty temper and make her scream bad words and send the blood rushing to her head until her face was puffy and flushed. Nothing enraged her more than to be called white. One day Inga got so provoked over this name that she stripped off her clothes and flashed the pum-pum spitefully at Service, chasing after him when he refused to look at it and be roused into a tormenting craving that she would not satisfy. Aloysius pleaded with Inga not to goad Service with the naked pum-pum unless she intended to dose him, but she snarled at him to mind his own business.

Stark born naked, she raced into the bush after Service, who was by then hiding in the crown of the tree. When she found him, she lay at the base of the tree and twined her legs up on the trunk so the pum-pum would be revealed in all its utmost and provoking glory. Service screamed and bawled insults and refused to look at the bared pum-pum. Aloysius caught up with them and begged Inga to come back to the house and stop tormenting Service. The tree bawled that it was a Christian tree and wasn't born into this world to hold up no pum-pum for nasty peep-show. Bushes raised a deafening clamour about Pum-Pum War reaching poor Jamaica.

There had even been worse rows than this one. Fists had flown at least once in the past week, and Service had been knocked senseless by a kung-fu kick.

But tonight there was a relative peace and the three of them were sitting around the fire and gabbling about Japanese, mushrooms, woman batty – the sun, moon and stars.

Inga kept bringing up Busha. She wondered what a white man was doing in this place, why he had such a big house and so much money, why he owned so much land when everyone around him was so poor. Aloysius said that it was all God's doing. Service said that there was no God, there was only mud.

"There is a God," Inga disagreed. "But he is not a conceited old man who must always have his own vay. Vhen ve don't do his vill, he brings us back to his vorld again and again. I have been back many times already."

"Mud is God," Service grunted.

"But I vill never do vhat he vants," she hissed. "He could bring me back a thousand times, he vill never make me do vhat he vishes. I vill do exactly vhat I vant to do. Do you know vhat he's going to have to do vith me to get his own vay?"

"Vhat?" Aloysius wondered.

"He vill have to kill me completely. But he can't do that because it would be admitting that I had won. So vhen I die he always sends me back to teach me another lesson."

"But Inga," Aloysius said after a pause, "vhy you just don't do what God vant? Is only right because God is your maker."

Her eyes blazed.

"Vhat am I supposed to be, some old man's toy? You think that's vhat my vhole life is for? To give some old man pleasure by scratching at his feet? Vhen he valks past this sheep in the pasture she bares teeth at him."

"Dat is foolishness," Service grunted. "Man is mud. Woman is mud. Pickney is mud. Goat is mud. Everything is mud. Parson is mud. De Governor General is mud. De Prime Minister is mud. De Queen o' England is mud. Bumbo is mud and pum-pum and hood is mud and everything else is mud. Mud, mud, and more mud. Dere is no God and dere is no coming back. When you dead you dead and gone back to mud."

"Everything that lives has a spirit. The spirit always comes back. Sometimes it comes back as an animal. Sometimes it comes back as a human. You kill a goat one day, and the next day it comes back as a baby parson."

"Listen!" Service said crossly. "When me kill a goat, it not coming back as no rass parson. Me is a butcher. Me is not a parson-maker."

"The life in the goat vill come back. All life comes back."

"Rass foolishness! Where you get dis stupid idea? You say so because you never kill a man. If you kill a man you know better."

"One time I put a bomb in a Paris restaurant that killed fifteen people."

"But you never kill a man up close."

"I killed a magistrate in Rome from ten feet away. I shot him in the head at a traffic signal. I saw him blink just before I put the bullet in his brain."

Service scuffed angrily at the ground.

"Why everything I do you must do one better?"

"Because I am a voman, and you are only a stupid man."

"Stupid man!" Service screeched. "You think me is a stupid man? Well, I kill one better dan you! I kill me father. You kill your father, too?"

"Me God, man!" Aloysius gasped. "Vhy you kill you Daddy?"

He reached over and touched Service sympathetically on the forearm.

Service pulled his arm fiercely out of reach.

"Don't touch me, you mad rass! Touch me and I chop up you bumbo!"

Inga said that she did not believe Service had really killed his father, that he was only boasting. Service swore that God could strike him dead if he was lying, and when God did not oblige, he said that it only went to prove he was telling the truth. Aloysius felt pity on any man who carried such a grievous sin on his conscience and was moved by the need to approach and touch and offer comfort. But when he moved closer, Service screamed that he would chop off the first mad finger that touched even a button on his shirt. Inga told Service to shut up, that if he laid a hand on Aloysius she would personally break it.

"Is all right," Service scowled. "Dat how white woman treat negar man in Jamaica. Negar man used to it by now."

"Don't call me a vhite voman, you bitch!" she hissed.

"Service," Aloysius pleaded, "you know dat Inga don't love that name. Vhy you call her so all de time?"

"What happen?" Service glowered. "Her skin not white? She not a white woman?"

"Call me that one more time and I show you something good!"

Service shrugged.

"Is all right. Me is a negar man. Me used to hard life and wicked treatment. Me no know 'bout anybody else. Me only know 'bout me. Me is a negar man."

"Me auntie used to tell me dat me Daddy was a Coolie," Aloysius boasted. "So me not whole negar. Me is only half."

"One thing 'bout tree," the tree cut in. "Tree no white, tree no black, tree no Chiny, tree no Coolie. Tree is pure tree."

"Same wid bush," a bush mumbled. "We is all one wid God family."

"Praise de Lord!" another bush cried.

"Hallelujah!" a third rejoiced in the distance.

All over the pastureland, other bushes took up the shriek.

"Bumbo," Aloysius moaned. "Dem think dis is a church."

"Now him hear bush talking again. Or tree," Service grunted. "Mad shit!"

They fell silent. Inga stared with longing and hatred at the lights from Busha's house.

"This is the vay God vorks," she said, pointing at the lights. "He plant a very rich man right among very poor people. He gives one child cancer and another child genius. He makes one voman beautiful and another voman ugly. Then he forces ugly voman to ride side by side in the same compartment of a train for thirty hours vith the beautiful one. I saw this once myself on a train. The ugly voman hid her face for shame and vouldn't look at the beautiful one. The beautiful voman polished her nails and read a magazine. I said to them, 'You know who is doing this, don't you? It's God.' 'Vat you mean?' the beautiful voman asked. I said 'Look at that ugly voman sitting across from you. You think this is coincidence that you take a train from Istanbul to Paris and right across from you is an ugly voman vhen you are so beautiful?' The ugly woman got mad at me and rang for the porter and complained that I insulted her. I said to the porter, 'All I said vas that she is ugly. Look at her yourself. Did I tell a lie?' The porter called a policeman. Vhen I explained to the policeman vhat I had said, he took me by the elbow and valked me to another compartment. 'Listen,' I told him, 'It's not my fault. It's God who does this. If I were God, I vould make everybody beautiful. I vould be a better God than the one ve have.' He laughed and said that he vas a Moslem and that he believed that everything vas God's vill also. 'My own vife is ugly,' he said. 'I always swore I vould marry only a beautiful voman, but then Allah made me to marry my brother's vidow, who is very ugly. Now even my children are ugly like their mother. But you can't discuss these religious topics on a train.'

"But that is God's vay: he always giving us tests just like a schoolmaster. He always grading, grading. In return he expects love, humility, and obedience. If he vere a human being ve vould say that he vas mad and put him in an institution for his own good."

"I goin' tell you how my God work," Service said. "My God is mud. Mud don't give nothing, mud don't take nothing. Mud don't make nobody sick and mud don't make nobody better. Mud don't listen to no preacher and mud don't hear no prayer. Mud don't want nothing except more mud. Mud love mud. Mud love mud so much dat all mud want in dis life is dat everything, everybody turn to mud. And sooner or later mud goin' get him way."

"Vhat you think, Aloysius?" Inga asked, turning to him where he sat hunched against the trunk of a tree, listening.

"Me brain confuse," Aloysius mumbled.

"What brain?" Service sneered.

"God do things dat me don't understand. Everyday me see him do things dat make me ask, 'Why you do dat, God? Vhy you bring trouble 'pon dat poor ole soul?' Vhen me was little boy, me auntie used to say, Aloysius, you have such a big brain. If you get a chance you bound to be a barrister.'

"But God never give me de chance to reach me ambition in life. God take me outta school before me learn to read and write.

"Den me grow little bigger and me see everybody 'bout me have a Mummy and a Daddy, me used to say, 'God, vhy me don't have a Mummy and a Daddy, too? Vhy all me have is one ole aunt? Vhere my Mummy, God? Vhere my Daddy?' But him don't answer me, Inga. Me talk to him till me run outta breath and him still don't answer me."

"Mud don't have tongue to talk to madman."

"God doesn't talk to his sheep. He only vants to hear them bleating at night. It helps put him to sleep like the sound of running vater."

"All me know is dis, Inga: God give me a big brain but him didn't give me a chance. But if me did get a chance me would be a good barrister. And if me did get a Mummy and a Daddy me would be a good son. Me vould be de best barrister and de best son in all Jamaica. A-hoa!"

Lost childhood, missed chances came flooding sorrowfully upon Aloysius, making him sob.

"Hush up you mouth, damn madman!"

"You shut up. Let him cry if he vants to cry."

"Why you must always stick up for him against me, eh? Why you must talk to me like me is a boy?"

"If he vants to cry he can cry. And if you don't like the vay I talk to you, you can go to hell."

"God do me plenty injury, Inga," Aloysius said in a broken voice. "But me not raising me hand against God. Him is still me Daddy."

They fell silent. The fire cracked the wood like a dog with a bone. Stars hung over the brow of the dark mountain, whose dim outline loomed in the thin blue night.

"I vill have to go home," Inga said finally. "There is no more money."

Aloysius leapt to his feet with alarm.

"No, Inga," he protested. "You can't go home. Ve is family here. Jamaica is you home. Right, Service? Dis is Inga home, eh?"

"Me no family wid no madman."

"All three of us can work, Inga," Aloysius continued hopefully. "Me can get a job with Busha, digging ditch. Service butcher goat. You can work too."

"I can't vork. I am a foreigner. Ve are not allowed to vork vithout permit."

"Look 'pon me, Inga. Six years now me live in de bush. It not hard. You have fruit to eat, you catch a crab here and dere, you eat fish. You can live so, Inga. Nobody get fat from dis life, but is life. You can get through."

"Busha sits upon that hill vith all his money vhile we stay down here vith nothing."

Service squinted at the lights burning outside Busha's house.

"Busha probably don't even lock up him door at night," he grunted.

Aloysius walked over to Inga and touched her gently on the shoulder.

"Inga, you mustn't go. What me goin' do without you, eh? You is de only family me have."

"Only pum-pum you mean," Service sneered.

"Shut up!" she snapped. "He is being sentimental. I like sometimes sentiment. Be sentimental vith me, Aloysius."

"Me not sentimental, Inga. You can't go home. Vhat me goin' do vithout you? Who me goin' have to tell joke to? Before you come is only me one and de tree and a whole heap o' bush. Who me goin' hold discussion with?"

"Who me goin' grind?" Service mocked.

"Aloysius!" the tree cried. "Me and you keep company. What happened? You don't like me company anymore?"

"But you is a tree!" Aloysius cried. "You good company, but you is a tree."

"Is because me don't have pum-pum," the tree said sullenly.

"No, man!" Aloysius replied.

"Is true!" the tree screamed spitefully. "All dem night and day dat you and me hold discussion everything all right. But now pum-pum come 'pon de scene, everything change us. Now everything is pum-pum, pum-pum, pum-pum. Aloysius, remember what de parson dem say 'bout pum-pum."

"Now you have de rass madman chatting to tree," Service scowled. "You mad up him brain again."

"Me not mad," Aloysius said. "De tree jealous."

"Jealous, you rass!" the tree screamed angrily. "Go 'way wid you damn pum-pum! Heaven is where me goin', and pum-pum don't cast no shadow dere."

Then the tree began to sing a shrieking hymn, spitefully. It was a raucous vulgar hymn that the tree had made up, one that screeched about crossing the River Jordon to the Heavenly Land where no Pum-Pum abounded and no Hood abided. The refrain was something about "Hood and Harp Keep no Company among the Heavenly Ewes."

"Lawd God, him goin' drive me mad wid de singing," Aloysius moaned, squatting again before the fire.

"Shut up vith that damn singing or I chop off another limb," Inga said to the tree.

"Now dis madman have you talking to tree too," Service said sourly.

"Inga," Aloysius moaned. "You can't leave me."

Another brooding stretch of silence fell over them.

"I am certain he has money up there," Inga hissed, glaring at the lights of Busha's house.

Service squirmed.

"Me broke five house in me day," he boasted. "House not hard to broke."

They fell silent. All around them the night grunted and hissed and wheezed its familiar cacophony. Insects and frogs wailed like lost children. Croaking lizards hawked in the dark treetops like nasty pensioners.

As the fire gnawed on the edge of darkness and no one spoke, some nameless, palpable and ancient thing drifted out of the night like a whiff of foul air and settled among them.

Aloysius sensed its presence first.

"Break Busha's house?" he cried suddenly. "Ve can't thief from Busha! Dat not right!"

Chapter Eighteen

It was like death, this thing that had come among them. It was a thing that they imagined could not happen even though they knew it would happen, a thing that they tried to ignore even though it was always on their minds, a thing that stalked between them morning, noon and night, that was always there but not there, like death, this thing that had now come among them.

It put fire in Inga's eye and a spring in her step and gave her a greater craving for hood so that she would slink off into the bush with one or the other of her two men sometimes three or four times a day until one of them was broken and the other complained of a bad back and she scowled around the small house kicking at its walls and pacing feverishly over the commons with this thing trailing after her.

Service kept the thing close to him like a selfish child clutching a favourite toy to its bosom and he sat outside the small house and sharpened and resharpened his knife and machete and longed for butchering jobs so he could give voice to the thing he felt in his heart, and eventually, restless and tired of idleness and pum-pum and carping at Inga, he went off into the bush, stole three chickens, chopped off their heads and sat grinning as the headless birds fluttered across the yard splattering a wake of blood in their maddening death dance.

The thing drew Inga and Service closer. It was his body she wanted now that the thing was among them. It was to him that she came in the morning, and at noon when he wasn't away butchering in the fields, and at night when the croaking lizards hidden in trees coughed up phlegm from their throats and filled the woods with their nasty sound, it was Service that she drew into the darkness with her.

Inga was the rider during this lovemaking. With the heat of the thing on her now she was always the rider, pinning her lover to the ground, clutching his wrists and holding him down in the spread-eagle position of crucifixion, and impaling herself on him with an anger and roughness and passion that made Service burn with resentment and wounded pride and caused him to flail and struggle under her during this lovemaking. The thing was like a fire inside her, a fire that she tried to quench with founts of fierce lovemaking, but when it was done and they walked back to the small house the thing would still be there was always, waiting.

Aloysius sulked and brooded during these days. He went into the bush alone and took long walks over unfamiliar pastures and down footpaths leading to distant villages. He talked to bushes and to trees and recited his thousand names to a curious lizard.

But the thing would be there too waiting for him when he came back to the small house.

And Inga would be there, with lust burning in her eyes. Service would be there, smouldering with hatred and discontent, temporarily useless as a man and despising Inga for making him so.

Sometimes Inga would then invite Aloysius into the bush where she would wreak passion on his private parts and bellow,

"O-lsopropoxyphenyl!" in his ear, leading him back to the house with a ringing in his ears and a deadness to his hood.

She could not get enough from these two during these first days when the thing shambled among them.

"Negar man not make for white woman to ride morning, noon and night," Service grumbled one afternoon when she wanted hood from him.

"Don't call me vhite voman!" Inga snapped.

She turned to Aloysius. He clambered unsteadily to his feet and followed after her. He did not feel like grappling with pum-pum or wriggling in the dirt under Inga but he could see that the thing was hard and fast upon her and that her heart was burning so he agreed to follow her because of pity and love.

"Aloysius!" the tree begged. "Come back! How much pum-pum you goin' get in one day? Pum-pum goin' kill you before de sun set tonight! Come back, you brute!"

"Is all right," Aloysius said wearily over his shoulder. "Me drink a bottle of Guinness stout yesterday."

"Stout, you bumbo! Stout can't help you now! Pum-pum goin' drain out you brain. Nothing goin' left inside but one empty shell. Come back, Aloysius, before pum-pum kill you stone dead!"

Aloysius wobbled after Inga into the bush, leaving the tree shrieking behind him like a disobeyed mother.

They were watching Busha's house now that the thing was upon them, watching it morning, noon and night. Whenever they heard a noise from the house – whether motorcar engine or dog bark or maid cough or door slam – one or all of them would turn and star like inquisitive fish at the hill on which Busha lived.

In the mornings they watched Busha and Sarah drive away from the house. They watched as an old gardener spilled out into the front yard and maids drifted onto the veranda trailing laughter and gossip behind them.

In the evenings they watched Busha come back from the fields, his pick-up smeared red with the rich dirt of his pastures, watched Sarah's car bump slowly up the driveway in a whining first gear.

They watched late into the night as the lights went out one by one in Busha's windows and two dogs romped on the lawn in a tangled skein of shadows cast by the harsh glare of a naked outdoor bulb.

For a whole week they watched Busha's house intently, without admitting what they were doing, without talking to each other about what they had seen.

One night as they sat around a fire stealing glances at Busha's house, the tree spoke out against this constant watching.

"De three of you watch Busha's house like mongoose watch fat chicken."

"Me not watching anything," Aloysius mumbled.

"Vhat? Vhat you talking about?" Inga asked.

"De tree say we watch Busha house too much."

"Tell him to mind his own business!" Inga grated.

"How tree can mind anybody else's business, eh? Him talk to tree. You talk to tree. Him talk to bush. You talk to bush. Stone, you bumbo." Service kicked savagely at a stone, "you chat too much! Moon, you rass, stop you singing! Sky, you blood, hush up you mouth! De two o' you drive me mad, too. Now, de three of us is ready for de madhouse!"

Inga chuckled.

Aloysius heaved a laboured sigh.

"Now see dis crosses on me head, now," the kicked stone wailed in the ensuing silence. "Missah Aloysius, you hear me say anything, sah? Me sit down on the dirty ground minding me own business when dis damn man kick me in me neck back and nearly burn me up in de fire. What me to him? Who me trouble? Dis is Jamaica for you! Where man treat man like dirt! God strike me down dead if I don't migrate to America next year!"

"Hush up you mouth!" Aloysius hissed, glancing uneasily at Service.

"Now who him hear chatting?" Service bellowed.

Aloysius shrugged lamely.

"Nobody."

"Me chatting!" the stone shrieked. "Me is somebody! Me is no nobody! Who you calling nobody, you mad rass?"

A light went out in Busha's bedroom window.

They turned and stared at the darkened house on the hill.

They would break Busha's house and thief money Busha thiefed from everyone around him. Busha hoarded this thiefed money in a safe somewhere in his drawing room because Busha hated bank worse than Pope hate pum-pum. So the money had to be in the house, hidden someplace where Busha could get it to pay his field workers, his maid, his headman who occupied a cottage on the edge of Busha's vast property. It would be wornout money, creased and grimy like an old labourer's hand, perfect money for theifing.

That was what they would do. Break open Busha's house and thief his money.

Aloysius moaned: He could not thief from Busha.

Why not? What had Busha done for him except roar past in his big car and splatter him on a rainy day? What kindness

had Busha ever shown Aloysius? If he was starving on the
roadside, would Busha give him an old fish to eat or a crust of
bread-back? What did Busha ever do for any man except
use him?

Aloysius squirmed. He couldn't thief from Busha.

Why not? Was Busha his family? His brother? Was Busha his
uncle or cousin? Busha was only a nasty white man with a red
face and a big belly who owned all the land in the district.
Busha thiefed from every man in the parish. Busha thiefed the
butchers who bought scrawny goats and cattle from him. Busha
thiefed the toothless old higglers who bought fruit from him to
peddle in ratty roadside stands. How else except by thiefing did
Busha get a big house on a hill, a chromed motorcar, a plump
wife, and all the land in the valley from the main road to the
foot of the mountains? Through thiefing, that's how Busha
got rich.

Aloysius stood his ground. Busha was a thief. But he,
Aloysius, was not a thief. He would not thief from Busha.

Then I must go home, Inga said. For I have no money.

Inga, Aloysius cried. Inga, don't leave me.

You and your damn tree can keep company in de dark night
form now on, Service gloated.

Aloysius, the tree cried, Is all right. We can talk just like me
and you used to talk before. Make dem go. Good riddance to
bad rubbish.

Inga, don't leave me alone!

Vhat you vant me to do? Eat grass like one of Busha's goats?
Is that vhat you vant me to do?

No more pum-pum, madman. Grind de tree next time you
hood stand up.

Who you talking to, you nasty ole negar? the tree screamed.
You think me is a battyman? You think me sleep wid odder

man? You nasty ole negar you! Is only bee dat me give grind to and dat's because dat is de plan of de Almighty.

Inga, me can't thief Busha.

Nobody is saying that you must do it. I vill go home. I said I vill go home. That is the end of it. There.

Inga.

Hush up you mouth, madman.

Inga, is a sin.

Don't do it, then, you fool. I already said I vill go home.

Sin, you bumbo! What you talking 'bout? Sin what? When mud thief from mud who mud sin against? Hush up wid you damn foolishness 'bout sin!

Inga, Busha and me play 'pon de same cricket side!

Vill you shut up! I told you, I vill go home! I vill not do anything you don't vant to do. I vill go home tomorrow.

Tomorrow, Inga?

You pum-pum goin' a foreign, madman. From now on you goin' grind bush.

Grind bush! a horrified bush screeched. Him not goin' grind no bush! Dere is no bush in Jamaica dat have pum-pum for madman to grind!

Grind bush! another echoed. Kiss me neck! Now dem want grind bush!

Grind bush! Grind bush! Grind bush! the refrain echoed across the land. See what Jamaica come to now! Now dem grinding bush! No madman goin' breed dis bush!

Me is only a poor bush! Me don't have no pum-pum!

Help! Police! Dem goin' grind bush now!

Me is a decent bush! Me not giving no madman a grind.

Inga!

Stop calling my name! It's settled. Tomorrow I go home.

Inga, don't go. Vhatever you say me do. Stay wid me, dat's all me ask.

No. you say you don't vant to do it. So ve von't do it.

Inga. Hear me. Vhatever you say. Vhatever. I do vhat you say.

Busha dog know you, madman? Me don't love dog bite.

Vait. Before ve go on vith our planning. Aloysius and I vill valk into the bush.

Why? Because de rass madman say him goin' do it right away you must give him pum-pum? Why?

Because I vant to. Now shut up. Aloysius?

Give him de rass pum-pum if you want to! Me don't give a rass! Go 'way wid de two of you!

Aloysius! Listen to advice from your best friend. Don't go, Aloysius! Don't go Aloysius!

Inga, me love you.

Shhh. You wriggle too much. Hold still.

Inga! You is me only family. You is de one person in de whole vorld dat love me.

Vill you stop it! I can't feel the hood with all your wriggling!

Me not wriggling. Me trying to tell you dat me love you.

You said that already, damn it! I don't like talking and wriggling vhen I'm in the middle of a fuck.

Me not wriggling.

Shut up, damn it!

Me not saying nothing.

O-Isopropoxyphenyl! O-Isopropoxyphenyl! O-Isopropoxyphenyl!

Inga, wid all me heart me love you.

Chapter Nineteen

Planning. Planning. Planning. That is the answer. Everything must be planned. They must plan who vill vatch vhat and who will do vhat. They must take everything into the plan. They must know who vill be in the house vhen and vhere. They must decide vhen they vill do it, vhere they vill enter the house, vhere they vill go vhen they are finish, vhere they vill hide the money. They must think like the police and get ready an alibi.

Alibi? Service wondered. What name alibi?

That is an explanation of vhere ve vere vhen the burglary occurred. So if the police ask us vhere ve vere, ve all have the same answer.

Why white people love so much plan, eh? You can't do nothing else but plan, plan, plan. You plan so much is wonder you do anything.

Don't call me vhite. I don't like that name.

All me know is dat me carrying me knife and machete with me. Dat's all me know.

Knife? Machete? Inga, vhy him need knife and machete?

Me don't break no house without me knife and machete.

Inga, ve not goin' hurt nobody, right? Ve only goin' get de money, eh?

I say that already. I don't like to repeat myself over and over again.

Aloysius, the tree said sadly, I can't believe you turn thief. See how you make pum-pum drag you down! I can't believe you turn thief right before me eyes.

Mind your own business. I not talking to you.

Tell dis rass madman to stop chatting to tree or I goin' get vex and chop it down!

Chop me down? You rass you, you can't chop me down wid no machete! Bigger man dan you can't chop me down!

Sunday evening is the best time. The maids are gone, and so is the garden boy. Busha and his vife go for their Sunday drive. The house is empty.

Thief on Sunday! No, Inga! Sunday is de Sabbath day!

Hush you rass mouth! Man can thief any day him want thief. Murder on Sunday. Thief on Sunday. Grind on Sunday. Tell lie on Sunday. Anything to rass you want do on Sunday.

Stop this idiotic arguing, both of you!

Me don't thief on Sunday, Inga.

Aloysius, you mean to tell me dat you really goin' thief on Sunday?

Mind you own business.

Him talking to de rass tree again! Where me machete? I goin' cut down the blood tree right now. Where me rass machete?

Shut up and sit down. Ve have a lot of planning to do between now and Sunday.

Dis Sunday, Inga? Dis Saturday is de cricket match!

Now him can't thief de day after cricket. Where you learn all dem rule from, eh? De madhouse?

I have a lot of planning to do. But I love to plan. Planning is vhat I do best. It puts me in a very good frame of mind to make a good plan. It makes me draw deep breaths and feel strong. I feel very strong now.

Don't bother look at me. Me not grinding no more white woman again today.

Vhite woman? You call me that name again? You vant to see I hold you down and take it out?

Hold who? Take what? You mad rass!

I show you who's mad.

Don't come near me! You think me is a rass country pickney you can hold down in de bush …

Inga, him don't want do nothing!

Lemme go, you rass white voman! Lemme go! Blood! Take you rass hand outta me pants! Lemme go!

Inga!

I goin' kill you bumbo if you do dis to me!

Inga, you goin' cause worries!

BUMBO! LEMME GO, WHITE BITCH! BUMBO! PUM-PUM BITE ME!

The plan went this way: Pretending to be going for a Sunday afternoon stroll, Inga would take the bush path that skirted the roadside and head towards Busha's house. Service would take the road.

Aloysius, meanwhile, would go ahead of Service. He would make sure that no one was watching then walk boldly up Busha's driveway. He would holler the house as though he were begging money or work and calm the dogs. If anybody was in the house, a maid or garden boy, Aloysius would ask for Busha, be told that he wasn't home, and return quickly to the road to warn Service. Then they would both signal Inga who would be watching from the bush and go back to their own house to make another plan.

But if the house was empty, Aloysius would lure the dogs into the garage and lock them inside. He would wait for Service and Inga to join him outside the house. They would then break into the house, find the money, put it in a bag, and leave separately and quickly.

Good timing would make this plan work. Service would have Inga's vristvatch. He would use it to time how long Aloysius had been in Busha's house. After five minutes he would assume that no one was at home and that Aloysius had locked the dogs in the garage.

Listen me, lunatic. You better can do dis in five minutes. If dog bite me, I goin' chop you rass. You hear me, sah?

Me can do it in five minutes. It not hard. De dog dem know me. Vhen me work for Busha, de dog dem used to sleep vid me.

Ve must rehearse it.

Rehearse? What name so?

Ve act it out. Ve rehearse. Ve pretend that this is Busha's house and Aloysius is coming up to it and doing vhat he has to do. Rehearse. That is vhat ve must do. Rehearse.

They rehearsed, but it went badly. Aloysius was not at ease. The first time he practiced how he would approach Busha's house he darted from bush to bush the way he'd seen a thief do in a movie.

"Busha! Hullo, de house!" he cried, as he scurried between the bushes. "Is Busha home, please? Busha!"

Inga burst out of the house and screamed at him.

"You must valk normal up the driveway," she bellowed. "Valk like a postman."

The tree chimed in.

"Honest man can't thief without acting like thief."

"Is true, you know," a bush agreed. "Me used to know a man who did thief one chicken, and from dat day to dis him walk sideways like crab."

Another bush agreed.

"If you thief you goin' walk like thief."

"Lawd, God," another bellowed, "dey practicing how to thief Busha. Who Busha trouble?"

"Hood fall off de fornicator," another bush screeched. "Thief walk like mongoose. De liar drown in him own spit. For thus saith de Lord, 'I put me mark o' iniquity on de body o' de sinner'."

Aloysius listened nervously to all the clamour around him.

"Inga," he pleaded, "vhy ve must thief on Sunday?"

"Vill you shut up about it and get on vith the rehearsal."

Aloysius retreated from the house until he was some distance away. Service hid behind a bush and began the timing.

This time Aloysius walked normally.

"Oyyyeaaah!" he called. "Busha! Please! Busha!"

"Thief, you bumbo!" a bush shrieked at him.

"Oyeaaaah!" Aloysius called, huffing and puffing like one climbing Busha's steep marled driveway. "Busha, please!"

"Busha not home! Go 'way, you damn thief!" the tree hollered.

"Me not thief!" Aloysius cried with shame. "Me love Inga."

With a hideous snarl, Service sprang out from behind the bush.

"Him talking to tree again! Him goin' land every one of us in de workhouse! How anybody can broke house wid a madman?"

"Rehearse more," Inga said gloomily.

So they rehearsed some more. Tramping up to Busha's imaginary driveway, timing Aloysius as he acted out calming down the imaginary dogs and penning them in the imaginary garage. Over and over again they went through the motions of what had to be done to thief Busha's money.

When Inga was satisfied she instructed them in fingerprints
and footprints. She explained what fingerprints were and said
she would go into Ocho Rios and buy them all three pairs of
cloth gloves and that once they were on Busha's veranda they
would put on the gloves and touch nothing in the house with
their bare hands.

"Fingerprints," Aloysius said, looking with wonder at his
finger. "Me never know me have fingerprints."

"No two fingerprints are alike. Vhen the police come, they
vill fingerprint Busha's house. But they vill not find our
fingerprints there because ve vill be veering gloves."

"Me fingerprints not like nobody else fingerprints?" Aloysius
asked wonderingly.

"No," Inga said. "So ve must vear gloves."

"Dat a good name for a man, you know," Aloysius marvelled,
looking at his fingers. "Fingerprint. Aloysius Fingerprint
Gossamer Longshoreman Technocracy Predominate Involuted
Enraptured ..."

"Shut up, you bombo!" Service screeched.

But Aloysius could not shut up. Once he had started to say
his thousand names he could not stop.

"Parliamentarian Patriarch Vendure Emulative Perihelion ..."

"I goin' cut you rass open!" Service roared, grabbing for his
machete.

Aloysius ran away into the bush screeching his names. He
came to a quiet spot where he sat down mumbling beside a bush.

"Dichotomy Intellectual Chaste Iron-Curtain ..."

"Lawd Jesus," the bush moaned, "why you send dis madman
to mad up me brain wid all dem name?"

"Linkage Colonialistic Dilapidated ..." Aloysius droned.

"You rass you," the bush hissed, "you think you is de only
one wid long name? Well, listen to de name of dis bush."

"Impracticable Loquacious Predilection Abomination ..."
Aloysius roared angrily.

The bush roared back.

"Bush, big bush, little bush, fat bush, thin bush, ugly bush,
pretty bush, red bush, bushy bush, leafy bush, gorgeous bush,
rass bush, bumbo bush, blood bush ..."

So it went in the hot afternoon sun with the two of them
shrieking names at each other a thousand times over.

Came Inga's orders about footprints. Neither Aloysius nor
Service wore shoes, and Inga said that this was very bad because
they would leave a footprint in Busha's yard that might lead the
police to them. She said that they should tear up an old shirt
and wrap it around their feet to smear their footprints.

So they did what Inga told them to do, tearing up an old
shirt and binding their bare soles with it. When they stepped in
the mud their wrapped feet left only a fuzzy mark behind which
did not match up with the print of their bare feet.

Inga kneeled and examined both prints closely. Then she
stood up with a grin.

"This vill drive the police crazy," she chuckled.

Aloysius sat down and unwrapped his feet.

"Lawd god," a bush screeched, "pum-pum make man wrap
him foot! Why oh why oh Lawd you invent pum-pum to
torment man so? Why you put pum-pum in dis world to make
honest man turn thief?"

Aloysius leaned gloomily against the tree's trunk.

"Get off me, you rass thief!"

Chapter Twenty

Busha was worried about two things nowadays. He was worried that he would not score even a single run in the cricket match. It would be an unbearable ignominy if the only white man on the side made a duck. The closer the match got the more this worry pressed on Busha's brain. He went to sleep worrying about being bowled for a duck. The first word that sprang into his head when he woke up in the morning was "duck". This was usually followed by a gloomy phrase such as, "Bowled for a duck," or "Caught for a duck," or "Stumped for a duck." All week Busha was restless over this worry. Sometimes in the middle of a peaceful country evening with Sarah the word "duck" would pop into his mind and he would jump up and pace about like a man possessed.

The next thing that was worrying Busha was that any day now he might drop dead and end up behind Shubert's shop in the graveyard he despised so intensely. His day in the hospital had taught him that he could pop off anytime, anywhere, anyday, anyhow. Then every goat, cow, and donkey that usually foraged in the graveyard would line up to empty their bowels on his head. He wouldn't even be cold in his grave before the deluge of doo-doo and wee-wee would begin. He would lie in his dark coffin listening to doo-doo thumping against his graveslab and there wouldn't be a damn thing he could do about it.

(HPL)

When Busha got an *idee fixe* in his head, it stayed there for a good while. In fact, it tended to grow and swell against his poor brain until it gave him a splitting headache. And no matter how he thumped the side of his head or jumped up and paced about or tried to think matters through, Busha would usually end up feeling helpless and miserable.

One morning Busha woke up and stared at the grey dawn light seeping through the window and made up his mind so violently and suddenly that he leaped out of bed, landed with a solid thump against the wooden floor and practically ran to the toilet.

A few hours later he was on his way to Kingston.

To Busha's mind Kingston was a nasty, dirty, loveless, noisy Sodom and Gomorrah plus a wicked Babylon all wrapped up into one, and he hated the place with such a passion that he stayed away from it as much as he could.

There was more scoundrel in Kingston, more thief, more whore, more gunman than anyplace else on earth. Only the hangman truly loved Kingston because that was where he got most of his business. Without the stream of Kingstonians tramping towards his gallows, he'd have to go out and work for a living in the hot sun like everybody else instead of snapping neckbone at two hundred dollar a head in the shade of Spanish Town prison walls.

Yet it was also a fact that no place on the island was better for a man to dead than Kingston.

Kingston had more graveyard than coop had chicken, had graveyard of every size, quality and amenity.

In Kingston a man did not have to be stuck in the ground like old turnip: he could preserve his bones in the smooth walls of a palatial mausoleum with angel statue blowing horn on the roof and a solid mahogany door barring donkey, goat, chicken, cow and dog.

For a long time now Busha had been hungering to buy a mausoleum for his family, but always Sarah had interfered. This time there was no stopping him. He intended to follow his own mind. Moneague graveyard was not going to swallow him up.

As he drove to Kingston, Busha had his chequebook in his back pocket.

The road Busha took to Kingston was an old road cut in the earliest days of the fallen Empire. It wound over a hard green mountain, lanced through a watery plain, skirted a gorge and parted the heart of an arid valley.

Busha cornered his way over Mount Diablo where he glimpsed from the heights a vast checkerboard plain with wisps of smoke coiling off burnt fields and scattered settlements clinging to the edge of green fields in the valley below.

He drove past children playing with homemade pushcarts, grown men loitering in front of shops. Fat country women perched on the roadside wall with naked babies wriggling in their laps.

As Busha drove with graveyard on his mind, occasionally he would hear snatches of jabbering voices, the blast of a sound system, the whiplash of domino bone on a backyard table.

Soon Busha was winding his way through a gorge where the sluggish Rio Cobre, bloated with silt and water plants, unwound its old green body down the mountainside like some nightmare serpent caught outdoors in the sunlight.

An hour later the swampy effluvium of Kingston's slums blew in through the wing window of the car and made his nose run.

The man Busha was going to see was scamp, scoundrel, and thief all rolled up into one. These were the right words, to

Busha's way of thinking, to sum up the disposition of a man who made his living off death. Yet this man, who was a fat Jamaican of Syrian descent, kept the best graveyard on the island. No goats wandered in and out of the tombstones in this Syrian cemetery. Donkeys were unwelcome as were cows and chickens. Bad dogs and watchmen patrolled day and night keeping out vandals and intruders.

Mr. Saarem, the proprietor, was born in Jamaica but of strong Syrian consciousness. He often ate raw mince for dinner and cooked his food with peculiar spices that made his breath smell like soup. He was renowned as a glutton and had a fat belly whose hairy rolls bulged through his shirt. He had gotten the idea for a perpetual care graveyard from America. In the years of the socialist government during which, in the opinion of Mr. Saarem, Jamaica went temporarily mad, he had lived in Miami and gained an appreciation for perpetual care. When he returned to Jamaica he quickly saw that the island needed a new kind of graveyard.

A Jamaican is like a man who lives on a ship: he looks constantly at sea. He pays scant attention to his own quarters, expecting landfall and firmament to loom in his vision at any God-given moment. He neglects, most grievously of all, his graveyards.

A prominent citizen could be dead one day, laid to rest with all due pomp and circumstance, and the next day donkey and goat would be munching on his wreaths. No matter where you go in Jamaica, the dead are uncared for in public cemeteries.

So Mr. Saarem was indignantly explaining to Busha as the two of them sat in the cemetery's office.

Busha relished this indignation because it matched his own sore feelings about what goats and cows and donkeys were waiting to do to his own appointed grave site behind Mr. Shubert's shop.

But, of course, there was Sarah, who wanted to be buried near Mummy and Daddy behind the stone church.

"We can move dem, Busha," Mr. Saarem said as though he couldn't see at all what the problem was about.

"As a matter of fact," Mr. Saarem continued, "I agree wid your wife. Families should be united. You don't want to bury one here and one there and scattershot everybody all over de place. All should bury in de same spot. Is only right."

"Move Mummy and Daddy!" Busha exclaimed.

"We move grave all de time, Busha," Mr. Saarem said coolly. "Is part of the service we give. We give full service, Busha. Full service."

"Too bad you don't have service dat make a man don't dead," Busha muttered.

"What you want to do, Busha," Mr. Saarem chuckled, "put me out of business?"

Busha thought about moving Sarah's Mummy and Daddy. But there was his Mummy and Daddy too. Then there was Uncle Herbert and Aunt Mae. Not to mention great uncles and grand aunts and cousins galore. Busha counted them off one by one to Mr. Saarem.

"How so much of you in dat one graveyard?" Mr. Saarem asked with evident astonishment.

"Is two hundred years of McIntosh lying dere," Busha said boastfully.

Mr. Saarem shook his head with wonder and said the word Busha was waiting eagerly to hear: mausoleum. A family with so much dead needed a private tomb where the deceased could be laid out with dignity in alphabetical, chronological, or geographical order, depending on Busha's preference. The alternative was to chuck the whole family in the ground higgledy-piggledy and leave them there until Judgement Day. But it was obvious that such a makeshift arrangement would not satisfy Busha, who was used to better.

"A mausoleum!" Busha marvelled, as though he had never heard such a word before.

"Let me show you what I mean, Busha," Mr. Saarem said.

Mr. Saarem bellowed for a boy to bring him some of the display books. The boy returned carting an armload of enormous books crammed with colour plates of mausoleums.

Busha was in seventh heaven poring over the books whose cloth covers gave off a faint whiff of mould. He saw more mausoleums than he had ever dreamed existed. Some were squat and flat-roofed and garnished with what struck Busha as fish-scale ornamentation on walls. Some had stone columns and roof-top statues, a pediment embossed with the family's coat of arms, and walls smothered under carvings of acanthus and fleur-de-lys.

Mr. Saarem pointed out specific features of each design.

"You notice, Busha," he remarked, "dat we don't have no naked batty angel in dis place. Yet you see it all de time in America. But here we cover de batty. To me it just looks more dignified."

Mr. Saarem took Busha inside one of the mausoleums and showed where the bones of a prominent family were alphabetically entombed in its walls.

"We do all de genealogical research for the family coat-of-arms, Busha," Mr. Saarem whispered.

Outside, the sun was broiling hot. But inside the mausoleum the air was damp and cool, and footfall echoed like hoof on macadamized road.

The opulence, the serenity of it all took Busha's breath away.

When they re-emerged in the hot sun, Busha had made up his mind. It had been made up years ago anyway. But now it was definitely and firmly decided. He would buy a mausoleum for his family. This was where his own earthly remains would be laid to rest.

They were taking one of the cement footpaths that discreetly wormed past rows of tombstones when Busha saw the only sight in the whole place that put him off. On the roof of a mausoleum was a black stone angel blowing a horn.

"What's dat negar angel doing up dere?" Busha asked astonished.

Mr. Saarem glanced at the angel and smiled.

"Black marble, Busha. It come straight from a quarry in Italy. It's specially treated to bring out the shine."

"Listen me, Mr. Saarem," Busha said. "I deal wid negar man every day of my life. When I dead de one thing I don't want sitting on me head is negar angel."

Mr. Saarem chuckled.

"Dat's de way dat family feel too, Busha. Dem nearly carry me to court over dat angel. But I show dem de purchase order dat dem sign: ebony cherub. Dem say dem didn't think about ebony meaning black. But ebony is black every hour of de day, every day of de week."

"Is it a white family?"

"Whiter dan you and me, Busha."

"What a life, eh?" Busha remarked mournfully. "You and your loved ones dead and bury in a nice place and for de rest of eternity negar angel blowing horn over you head. If it was me, I'd paint it rass white."

At the end of the day, one of Busha's two worries had been lessened. He had signed a cheque for ten thousand dollars and authorized the cemetery to draw up plans for a family mausoleum and to do a genealogical search of his family's coat of arms. With one stroke of his pen, he had freed himself of the scabby Moneague graveyard. The only thing that could ruin his plan was if he died between now and when the mausoleum was built. He was therefore driving cautiously, staying well under fifty and keeping his eyes warily on side roads where cars and trucks had a way of popping out in front of you.

But in his hearty he knew that he had only transmogrified one trouble to another. There was still Sarah to be faced and her hard-headed opposition to a Kingston burial to be overcome. Busha hadn't the faintest idea how he would break the news to her, but he was grimly bracing himself for a hard and bitter fight.

Then there was also the prospect of the duck ahead of him. The duck was implacable, merciless, ruled by fate, and immune to chequebook.

If it lay in his future, money was powerless to stop the duck.

Chapter Twenty-One

It was Saturday morning of the big cricket match and Busha was grimly at bat. The first ball bowled to him was a wicked inswinger that bounded towards his unprotected head at some 100 miles per hour. Busha took a desperate slice at it with the bat and missed by a mile. He spun in his tracks, certain that he would see the stumps of his wicket go flying. But the ball zoomed over the bails and plopped harmlessly into the gloves of the wicket keeper, who immediately appealed that Busha had nicked it.

"Hoowwzzhhee?" the wicket keeper roared.

The umpire, a parson from a neutral mountain village, turned up his nose scornfully at the appeal.

Muttering under his breath about thiefing umpiring parsons, the wicket keeper returned the ball to the fast bowler, who began leisurely pacing off his length.

The sun beat down on Busha's head like a teacher's switch. He was dressed in the garb of the cricketer: he had on his whites; his legs were ensheathed in thick pads, his testicles baking in a protective metal cup. His fingers sweated under the rubber bristles of the batting gloves. On top of everything else his throat was dry and his belly hung off him like a dead weight.

Twenty-two yards from where Busha stood nervously at the wicket waiting for the fast bowler to reach his mark, Dr. Fox, the other opening batsman, smiled encouragingly at him.

The sidelines of the playing fields were thick with spectators. They spilled out over the boundary lines and dripped from the limbs of surrounding trees; they gawked from thick hillsides and peeped from car tops. Parasols bloomed thick in the air like wild flowers. Women were resplendent in their best dresses. Men had squeezed calloused feet into leather shoes and now pranced on the sidelines like newly shod horses. Everyone smelled of Saturday-night baths and Sunday morning scents.

The children had caught the excitement in the air and danced around their mothers, poking their heads through the thick crowd to ogle the cricket pitch. A babble of voices rose and crested and broke, punctuated by occasional laughter and shouts.

The fast bowler, a beefy cultivator from Walker's Wood who was usually murder on the Moneague batsmen, had reached his mark. He turned, pawed at the ground like an enraged bull, took a deep breath that blew him up to a frightful size, and began cantering towards the crease where he would deliver the ball.

Busha crouched and waited, his breath coming in sharp spurts.

"Duck" popped into his mind just as the bowler hurtled down on him, whipping a vicious bouncer towards the wicket.

Busha closed his eyes and swung the bat like an axe. The seasoned wood clouted the ball and sent it sailing over the boundary lines to carom off the asphalt road.

The umpire's arms stiffened into the air, signalling that Busha had hit a six.

The crowd bellowed deafeningly with one enormous mouth.

Padded and waiting his turn at the wicket, Mr. Shubert was sitting with the other batsmen and talking over his shoulder to

$78.59, who stood behind him shielding her head from the hot sun under a gaudy parasol.

In the eyes of the world $78.59 was a good-natured, big-batty widow who had eight grown children, lived in an unelectrified mountain settlement where she minded goats and chickens and was known to God and her neighbours as Mrs. Sepole. But because of tension Mr. Shubert could not remember the old lady's name, although he clearly recalled that her balance in his credit book was $78.59.

On all sides was Mr. Shubert hemmed in by other figures from his book. To his right was $130 dressed in a serge suit and putting on airs for a flirtatious young woman. Two rows deep behind Mr. Shubert, standing side by side, were $55.23, $98, and $210, who was in arrears and needed a good dunning. Before becoming aware of Mr. Shubert's presence, $210 had been blaring out to the whole world his vainglorious opinions about cricket. But one glimpse of the shopkeeper had caused the wretch to lower his voice and skulk away into the thicket of cloying bodies.

It was all in Mr. Shubert's book – the whole sorry story of the village – and only he knew the truth. Only he knew that the one over there with the big mouth carrying on like a fowl that just lay egg was down in the book for $86.29. Only he knew that a certain sister sweating under crinoline and umbrella on the sidelines and holding her head high like she was bound to go to heaven owed the shop $126.78 mainly for white rum purchases.

No matter where the shopkeeper looked, he could immediately pick out a face in the throng that owed him money. Even the fast bowler, now pacing off his fearful length, was down in the book. It was a comfort to Mr. Shubert to realize that no one, with the exception of Almighty God who had every name down in the Book of Life, kept more complete accounts on this horde of people.

"Mr. Shubert," a voice from behind sang pleasantly, "we expect a good knock out of you, you know, sah. You mustn't let us down today."

Mr. Shubert turned and looked into the homely brown face of a scrawny village woman whose husband operated a bus. He smiled wanly and mumbled that he would do his best.

$98.67, thought Mr. Shubert, as he settled down again in his chair. And come to think of it, the wretch had missed her payment last week.

The crowd thundered as Busha hit another towering six.

But Busha's heroics earned him no glory. For in cricket it is written that the properly stylish batsman should drive the ball low and humming over the turf where it can't be caught, should do so while striking iconic poses for the benefit of spectators and wearing a mien of effortless imperturbability like a Colonial English governess making doo-doo on the potty.

None of this is possible if one is hitting sixes. It requires such a wrenching effort of brute strength that the batsman invariably looks rude and clumsy. It is all too American and vulgar. A roar from the partisan crowd no doubt, but no appreciation whatsoever from the connoisseurs.

So Busha was applauded but not valued. He appeared to some sideline critics to be wielding his bat like it was a machete and he was a garden boy chopping grass.

Busha swung viciously at a yorker and sent it flying for another six.

"All dis rass white man can do is hit six," a spectator grumbled.

"Him think him butchering cow," another remarked.

"Dem soon bowl him," scoffed a third.

"Him swinging blind, dat's all," muttered another.

Moneague wickets began falling steadily all around Busha. Dr. Fox was stumped for one run and had to shamble off the field looking like he'd been caught thiefing a chicken. Mr. Shubert came in and was immediately cleaned bowled for a duck. As he was walking off doing his best to look dignified, Mr. Shubert paused to remind the bowler about the balance he owed the shop. The bowler got vexed and answered with a bad word.

Mr. Shubert muttered uglily that sooner or later the bowler would want credit again at which time his goose would most certainly be cooked. The bowler sneered that it was duck that was cooked not goose, a taunt which goaded Mr. Shubert into such an abusive tirade that the umpire had to walk over and order him off the field of play.

The spectators from Walker's Wood jeered the shopkeeper with a loud quacking as he took the long humiliating walk to the sidelines.

"Better luck next time, Mr. Shubert," $98.67 muttered to the shopkeeper as he sat down and began tearing off his pads.

Mr. Shubert turned on her savagely.

"How come you miss you payment last week?" he bellowed.

The woman blushed with shame.

"Lawd, Missah Shubert, sah," she whispered, "is not me bowl you, you know, sah."

By noon the Moneague side was in collapse. Busha was grimly hanging on to his wicket with a score of forty-six. He had belted five sixes over the parked cars. One had landed in the bush of the church graveyard and the ball nearly lost. But it was found under a mass of tendrils smothering a weathered graveslab and returned to play.

Aloysius, the last batsman on the side, came to bat barefoot and clad in a crushed pair of white pants that Busha had lent him. Busha's belly was so much bigger than Aloysius's that the waist of the pants had had to be fastened with an old necktie, which drooped down the seams like an ill-fitting cummerbund.

The captain of the Walker's Wood side flew at the umpire and protested a madman being used by the other team.

"Damn out of order, man!" the captain raged, "We have madman in our village too, you know, sah! I could fill me side wid a whole lunatic asylum if I had a mind to. But dis is supposed to be a friendly game! You don't use you madman in a friendly game!"

"Play de game, man," the umpire snapped. "Nothing in de rule book 'bout madman."

The captain retreated to his fielding position, muttering threats about next year filling his team with eleven raving lunatics.

Aloysius stroked a long four through cover point on the next ball. The next delivery he lofted towards the long-on boundary where it was gingerly caught by a fielder.

Just like that the side was all out for 95 runs.

There was a break for a curry goat lunch served under a Poinciana tree. Everyone on the Moneague side admitted that things were looking grim. The players tried to cheer each other up, but in spite of all the heartening words mumbled through mouthfuls of chewed goat, a thick gloom had settled upon them. Across the field, where the Walker's Wood side ate its lunch, there was a constant sound of lighthearted banter and laughter. Jokes were being told in boisterous voices and greeted with squeals and backslapping.

The same contrasting moods had settled over supporters of the two teams. On the Moneague sidelines a fight broke out during which a woman held down her husband and flogged him with a switch. Three special constables had to drag them both away to the police station accompanied by a frightful hissing from the unruly crowd. Children were cuffed, scolded and occasionally gave vent to an animal shrieking. Men were drinking themselves into a stupor. Women squabbled over old grievances.

But on the Walker's Wood side, there were no shrieking children, no fighting women, no drunken men, the crowd was in a jovial and happy mood. Laughter occasionally floated over the background jabber of voices. So many people scaled a lignum vitae tree, jostling for a place on an overhanging limb, that it broke with a loud snap and sent a mass of bodies tumbling headlong into the thick of the crowd. But even this accident was greeted with good-natured laughter as the fallen spectators picked themselves up off the ground, dusted off and began anew a scramble up the tree trunk.

A drunken woman, her eyes afire with rum, her voice thick and slurred, elbowed her way to where the dispirited Moneague team sat.

"You say you name cricket players?" she shrieked at the subdued men. "Is so you name? Cricket players? Well, listen me now, if you don't win dis game, we goin' ration pum-pum on you like de socialists used to ration butter. You hear me! No pum-pum for you if you don't win!"

A few of the bystanders sniggered at her antics, some scowled and muttered under their breaths. But most of them just looked away and shuffled their feet with painful embarrassment.

The players sat under the tree toying with blades of grass, twirling their shoelaces, or staring idly at the lines of spectators that twined thick and colourful over the hillside, draped off the branches of the surrounding trees, and curled over the eaves of neighbouring rooftops.

After lunch the Walker's Wood side stepped to the crease and began hammering the Moneague fast bowlers. The batsmen immediately drove the new ball to the boundaries for two fours. By the time the pacemen had worn a scuff into the new ball, the score was thirty-one runs for no wickets.

A water boy came on the field and the players took a short break for belly-wash and bullah cake.

"No pum-pum for de whole o' you!" the nasty drunken woman bellowed from the sidelines.

"I goin' get a constable to lock up her rass," the inspector glowered.

"Leave de damn drunk woman, man," Busha mumbled. "She just telling de truth."

"Let's just do our best and lose honourably," the parson counselled.

" 'Honourably' you bumbo!" Dr. Fox snapped. "We goin' be de laughing stock of de parish."

Busha inspected the ball to see whether it was sufficiently worn to bring on the spin bowlers. Then he tossed it to his best spin bowler, who was Aloysius.

The strategy in cricket is dictated by the condition of the ball. A new ball is hard and shiny like a marble, slippery to the grip and cannot be delivered with any appreciable spin. But the fast bowler can bowl it with tremendous speed, get it to carom wickedly off the pitch, and take wickets by scaring the daylights out of the batsman.

After the fast bowlers have had their innings, the ball becomes scuffed and worn, its seams raised and rigid like an old man's veins. Then the spin bowlers come on for now they can grip the ball and spin it with a flick of the wrist, making it arc through the air with tantalizing slowness and jink erratically at the stumps.

The pace of the game slows. The fielders draw perilously close to the batsman. The wicket keeper's gloved hands hover inches over the wicket. Deceit and swindle hang heavily in the air. Sudden death lurks for the unwary batsman.

"How you do today?" Aloysius murmured to the ball as he paced off his two-step length.

"Ahh me son!" the ball replied. "Times hard 'pon me. Me back nearly broke wid all de licking dem give me."

"De bat hard, eh?" Aloysius asked sympathetically.

"Hard!" the ball became indignant. "Hard, you rass! You don't know 'hard' yet? You should be born in a world where people batter you up wid a piece of wood, den you'd know 'bout 'hard'."

"Is true, you know," Aloysius muttered.

"Where dat white man? Him not batting now?" the ball asked anxiously.

"No, man. Him 'pon we team."

"Him nearly kill me Puppa wid all dem six. Hard knock to rass!"

The captain of the opposing team, who was at bat, strode angrily over to the umpire.

"De man is talking to de ball!" he bellowed. "Dey bring a madman to bowl us! What kind a thing is dis? Out of order to bring a madman to bowl us!"

On the sidelines the indignation was echoed by the supporters of Walker's Wood.

For the sake of peace, the umpire strolled over to Aloysius and asked him to please refrain from talking to the ball while he was bowling since it distracted the batsmen.

Aloysius took his mark.

His face wreathed in a ferocious scowl, the captain of the opposing team assumed his batting stance, slapping the tip of his bat angrily against the crease.

The crowd quietened down expectantly.

Aloysius took two steps and let the ball go. It floated high in the air, landed three feet outside the wicket, then darted like a snake at the stumps. Fooled by the sharp break, the captain mistimed his swing and nicked the ball into the hands of the fielder crouching at first slips.

"Howzzeee he?" the team roared.

The umpire's finger stabbed the air, signalling an out.

The fury of the captain was uncontrollable. He ranted and raved at the umpire.

Moneague had emptied its lunatic asylum to come and bowl against their team, the captain bawled, and here they had been decent enough to leave their own demented citizens behind. The umpire took a dim view of the clamour and ordered the irate captain to leave the field and bring on the next batsman.

Scowling ferociously, the captain stormed off to a hail of applause from his own crowd and a chorus of boos from the Moneague supporters.

The next batsman marched bravely to the wicket. He tidied up the crease, got the umpire to give him mid-stump, sniffed suspiciously at crouching fielders, and turned to face Aloysius with a threatening glare.

The first ball uprooted his leg stump.

The Moneague crowd exploded in a wild thundering of joy.

With the help of obeah, the devil, and lunacy (according to the captain of the other side) Aloysius took all wickets like they had never been taken before. He got a hat trick by clean bowling three. He got one for leg before wicket. Two others were caught.

The solid centre of Walker's Wood batting order where were planted three big-belly batsmen of enormous size and a gluttonous appetite for scoring, fell meekly for fewer than twenty runs. Every falling wicket brought the captain of the Walker's Wood team raving onto the field. Bad words flew out of his mouth like bats from a cave. He stormed up and down at his own players, screaming at them for being fooled and frightened by a madman. He protested to the umpire, the heavens, the spectators. He popped oaths and blasphemies and named some private parts old women on the sidelines had not seen in years.

But nothing he did or said made any difference. It still rained wickets. And when Aloysius was not bowling Parson Mordecai was wreaking havoc with his googly ball – one that bounced trickily and lured two batsmen out of their creases to a merciless stumping.

The final two wickets fell in quick succession. One batsman was running out as he tried to scratch two runs from a ball driven weakly past the mid-on fielder. The last man at bat, the beefy cultivator who was Walker's Wood fast bowler, hit a mighty six on his first swing, and popped up the ball to the long-on fielder on his second.

A tremendous roar erupted from the Moneague supporters, who surged onto the field, engulfing the players in an ocean of flailing limbs.

Moneague had won the game by twenty runs.

Late that night Aloysius straggled past the glare of the last street light in the edge of the village and tramped his way slowly up the empty and unlighted country road with crickets hissing in his ear and croaking lizards groaning at the darkness.

He had been overwhelmed by the crowd, carted off bodily to the nearest bar, and drenched with glass after glass of free white rum. The sound system had been turned up to its loudest volume and the vibrations of the reggae rhythms had pounded all evening through his body giving him a splitting headache. He had been hailed and slapped on his back and celebrated and told jokes like never before in his life.

The drunken woman had caught up with him and hauled him into a backyard where she dropped her panties and attempted to reward him with pum-pum on the roof of a rickety chicken coop. But even while Aloysius was groggily trying to make her understand that he could hardly stand up straight because of his great weariness, she passed out and fell on the ground, causing the penned chickens to explode in a noisy cackling.

Now, as Aloysius slowly scraped his way up the dark road, his eyes picking out the familiar shapes of trees and the low outline of the wall, he was aware that a sinister silence had descended on the darkened woods and fields. No bushes, no trees called out his name as he passed. The only sound he heard were the shrieking of the insects, the cries of frogs, and the hawking of the lizards.

He climbed over the wall and by starlight followed the narrow path that wound into the thick bushland where he had lived for many months alone with only the flame heart tree for company.

Inga and Service had not come to the cricket match. Inga said she did not understand cricket. Service said he had no use to watching grown men play a child's game.

Sitting on the stoop of the house, they would be waiting for him in the faint glow of the kerosene lamp.

On the night wind he could hear the sound of a file whetting a blade. It made the noise of an old man grinding his teeth during a bad dream.

Chapter Twenty-Two

So now it was Sunday. The day dawned bleak and overcast, and the grey light leaching through the clouds was watery and thin like weak porridge.

On Sundays the bushland always echoes with sounds of singing, chanting and hand-clapping mingled with distant preaching. Now these sounds wafted over green hills on a morning breeze and drifted down to the small house where Inga, Aloysius and Service waited, lost in thoughts.

Service sharpened and resharpened his machete. Aloysius stared gloomily at the dirt watching ants come and go. Inga wrote feverishly in her notebook.

They did not speak.

Busha and Sarah went to Sunday service and, as bad luck would have it, ended up sitting right behind the widow Dawkins who had sickly bowels and broke wind like Satan himself when she was in church. Once before Busha had sat beside the widow and she had very nearly blasted him to the rafters with her incessant farting. Since then he always made it a point to sit as far away from her as he could.

But this morning the widow was late. Only after Busha and Sarah were firmly wedged between a solid mass of portly matrons did she wriggle into a pew and settle down directly in front of them.

"Good God!" Busha moaned.

"Shhhh!" Sarah hissed between clenched teeth.

"Make we move, beg you!"

"We can't move. Service beginning."

"Lawd, God. I dead today."

Sarah jammed him hard in the ribs with her elbow.

Busha remembered where he was and began trumpeting *Rock of Ages*.

The bellowing of a distant preacher drifted down to the small house. Inga, Service and Aloysius could not make out the words, but the sound of the voice was harsh and angry.

"Me know what him saying," Service muttered, rasping the file against the silver grin of the machete. "He say pum-pum cause famine, stunt growth, make bridge collapse, make bus run late, give flour weevil, bring mosquito, cause drought and toothache. Pum-pum shrivel up toe, dry up eyeball, make barefoot man step on rusty nail and get lockjaw. No matter what war and trouble in dis world, parson say pum-pum cause it."

"How you know that's vhat he's saying? You can't hear his vords."

"Me know," Service muttered. "Me Daddy was a parson. When I chop him, he says, 'Is pum-pum make you chop me.' Dat's how parson mind work. Everything is pum-pum fault."

Inga got vexed, wriggled out of her pants, stripped off her panties, and sat naked on the stoop of the small house with her bare knees gaping wide at the grey sky.

"I vish my pum-pum was a flag," she growled. "I vould hoist it on a flagpole for every parson in the vorld to see."

Aloysius got up and paced moodily around the house, settling down with a sigh in the same place he had just been sitting.

It is a slow day in Jamaica, this Sunday. It drags like ground lizard through tall grass. The shops and bars are shuttered tight, the radio filled with sermonizing and hymn singing, the roads empty of people and buses, the fields stripped of workers. This dreariest of all days tightens like a hangman's noose around joy and laughter, reminds the old of dark nights and sends children scurrying nervously into the laps of clucking aunts.

A Jamaican Sunday sticks in the throat like fish bone. By noon even a pious heart hungers for the grim normalcy of Monday.

For the last time Inga went over fingerprints and footprints. Still naked, she crouched on the grass, her pum-pum gaping wide like fish mouth. Aloysius and Service sat nearby listening as she explained what they had to do.

Tears came to Aloysius's eyes.

"Vhat's the matter vith you?" Inga asked.

Aloysius hung his head.

"Him 'fraid," Service sneered.

"Shut up! Vhat's wrong, Aloysius?"

He hesitated.

"Yesterday me was de star of de cricket game," Aloysius said.

"Pickney game!" Service scoffed.

"Me take six wickets."

"So vhat? Vhat is your point?"

"Nobody say nothing to me! Nobody ask me how de game go? Me take six wickets! Me was de star!"

"Star you neckback!" Service sneered. "Pickney game."

"Shut up!" Inga snapped.

She looked at Aloysius.

"How vas the game yesterday, Aloysius?"

Aloysius sniffed.

"Me take six wickets," he mumbled.

"Is that good? To take six?"

"Dere's only eleven man on de side. Dat's very good."

"Then, congratulations."

She patted him on the head and stood up.

Her eyes were burning with a fierce light. She shook herself all over like a wet dog.

"I feel vunderful!" she crowed. "I feel like I vas just born!"

Busha and Sarah set out that afternoon on their Sunday drive. Busha almost always started out on the road that wound through Walker's Wood and led to the seacoast. Sometimes he would turn off onto a lane that climbed up the side of a mountain and snaked through sleepy hillside villages whose shops and houses wore the grim rectitude of Sunday. Or they would drive slowly on a ridge road that overlooked a view of placid green fields and big-cheeked mountains bulging against the skyline.

When they had small children these Sunday drives were the cause of much bickering and squabbling in the back seat with frequent stops for wee-weeing and spankings. But now that their children were grown and gone the Sunday drive had become for Busha and Sarah a moment of middle-aged peacefulness. They went where the whim took Busha, talked idly about everything and roamed the lands as if it were a windless green lake over which they were paddling a rowboat.

This Sunday Busha took the mountain road, climbing the summit in first gear. Sarah especially loved this road because of wild orchids that bloomed on the clay hillside and scented the air.

But any pedestrian who happened to see the car wind slowly past would have quickly spotted that all was not well inside, that the man was gesticulating like one pleading a hopeless case, and the woman's face cemented with the obduracy of a hardened old wife.

The car screeched to a stop on the summit.

"I not moving Mummy and Daddy!" Sarah cried shrilly, her voice piercing the stillness of the countryside. "You could talk till you blue in de face! I burying in Moneague beside dem!"

"You don't even give me a chance to explain!" Busha begged.

His face was turning blue.

The white woman and the two black men drifted up from the bushland on different paths towards Busha's house.

Aloysius went by the road, walking with an exaggerated air of nonchalance. He did not have far to go but still the distance seemed interminable to him. He was sure that eyes were following his every move and he turned frequently and looked about him as though to surprise a hidden observer crouching behind a nearby bush. He tried singing to calm fears, but his voice was nervous and squeaky. Not far behind him on the other side of the road, Service followed, a machete hanging between his fingers of his left hand.

Inga shadowed them on the bush footpath that ran parallel on the road.

Aloysius came to Busha's driveway and stopped. He looked over his shoulders, peered into the enormous fields that spilled out on either side of the roadway, and hesitated.

Service sat down on the stone wall. Inga slunk behind a bush.

Aloysius took a deep breath and started up the driveway.

"Oyyeaaah, the house!" he sang out, "Busha, please!"

Barking furiously, the dogs bounded down the driveway to meet him.

Busha and Sarah were quarrelling on the top of her favourite hill.

"Whenever I want anything in dis world, you block me!" Busha was raging. "Once you hear dat I want something, you say to yourself, 'Blocking time now!' No matter what it is! If I want to go here, you want to go dere. If I want dis for dinner, you must want dat! Blocking your husband! Dat's all you know how to do!"

"You not burying me in no dirty Kingston!" Sarah snapped. "You not uprooting Mummy and Daddy like is rose bush you transplanting. I don't care if de coffin lined with gold, frankincense and myrrh and de King of England bury beside me, you not doing it! And you can put dat in you pipe and smoke it for dat is final!"

"God Almighty," Busha rolled his eyes to heaven for help. "You see dis cross you give me to bear? You see how dis damn woman spend her whole life defeating me? Who wear de pants in dis damn family, anyway? Since when you is boss over me?"

"You could wear a hundred pants, you still not burying me in no Kingston. I burying in Moneague, where I was born, where I was a child, where I live my whole life!"

"I give Mr. Saarem a $10,000 downpayment! Because of you stubbornness, we goin' lose $10,000! Be reasonable, woman!"

"Dat is your business! I never tell you to sign paper to buy a mausoleum! Did I tell you to do dat? If you want to bury in dat place, go right ahead! But I bury where I spend my life – in Moneague!"

Busha started up the car.

"Well, nobody putting me in Shubert's backyard for goat and cow to do number one and number two on me head! I buying a mausoleum in Kingston and dat's where dey goin' bury me. And when I'm dere for once in me life I won't have you beside me nagging me head off! Thank God!"

"Buying mausoleum!" Sarah spat with contempt. "All of a sudden de place where him live him whole life is not good enough for him. You're a joke!"

The car took off with a violent jerk as Busha looked for a place to turn.

"No matter what I say, dis woman is against it!" Busha raged. "Opposition, opposition, opposition! Dat's all dis woman know! She should be in politics."

It struck Inga that Busha's house was like the abandoned lair of an animal. There was the spoor of an alien presence everywhere she turned: a crumbled newspaper was open on a coffee table in the drawing room, a half-drunk cup of tea sat on a side-board, dishes soaked in the sink. The musty smells of bodies hung warm and stale like dead air in every corner. Pictures and portraits of living and dead McIntoshes stared fixedly at her from the walls.

"Where Busha keep him money?" Service whispered.

"Behind dat picture on de wall," Aloysius replied.

They shifted the pictures and found a recessed wall safe. Service tried to pry it open with his machete, but the thick wooden door would not give.

"Ve need something stronger," Inga snapped. "Aloysius, see vhat you can find in the kitchen!"

Aloysius rushed to the rear of the house.

"Look at that fat pig up there!" Inga said, pointing to an ancient oil portrait of a portly, bewigged gentleman caught in a contemplative pose holding a book.

She went to the sideboard, grabbed the half-empty cup of tea, and hurled it at the portrait.

The cup shattered against the ancestor's ruffled ascot.

Busha drove like a man demented, his eyes fixed on the road, his face creased with anger lines. He tore through Walker's Wood, careened around corners, and roared past slow-moving buses on the few straight stretches of roadway.

"You kill yourself today in dis car," Sarah said tartly, "and I goin' bury you tomorrow behind Shubert shop."

"Don't bother talk to me!" Busha roared. "Just don't bother talk!"

"I talk if I want to!" she snapped. "I don't pay license on my mouth."

The scenery flashed past in a smudge of green. Busha stepped on the gas, honked to scatter a flock of browsing goats, and raced down the road leading to Moneague.

He blew through the village, blasting chickens and dogs out of his path with his horn, causing Sunday strollers to turn and peer with astonishment after him.

Then he was skidding past the quiet graveyard and barrelling down the quiet country lane on which they lived.

The car roared up the gravel driveway and ground to a screeching stop under the portico.

Busha bounded out, slammed the door after him and stalked angrily over the veranda and into the drawing room.

In the middle of the room he suddenly stopped dead in his tracks, the hairs on the back of his neck slowly rising.

The wall safe was torn open. Its thick wooden door hung like an idiot's drooping lip. Money was scattered across the floor.

"Sarah!" Busha flung over his shoulder. "Stay outside! Something goin' on!"

He was cautiously approaching the safe when murder reared up before him in a blur. Busha caught a glimpse of an upraised machete and instinctively lifted his arm to shield his head.

The machete slashed into his forearm with a hollow whack, and Busha crumbled on the floor with a moan.

Then Service was stooping over him struggling with the handle of the machete. He gave a grunting wrench; the blade popped out of Busha's bone with a splattering of blood.

Sarah screamed and rushed into the room as Service took aim at Busha's unprotected head.

"No kill Busha!" Aloysius howled.

He hurled himself at Service and drove him off his feet.

The two black men wrestled on the floor. They slammed into furniture and tumbled against a wall.

"Let him go, you fool!" Inga yelled. She grabbed Aloysius in a hammerlock, and pulled him off.

Service jumped up, grabbed the machete and uncoiled a vicious blow at Busha, who was trying to clamber to his feet but had slipped and fallen in his own blood.

A deafening explosion roared through the room. Service was flung against a sofa as though he had been thumped from behind by a fist.

He stood up and turned around slowly, a thread of blood unwinding down the side of his mouth.

From the doorway Sarah took aim at him with a revolver.

"She shot me!" Service bawled.

He put his hand to his chest. Blood oozed through the shirt and seeped between his fingers.

"Lawd Jesus!" he cried, dropping the machete and clutching his chest with both hands. "Lawd God, she shot me!"

Inga made a move as if to attack.

"I'll kill you stone dead," Sarah shrieked.

Tears streamed down her face, and she drew breath in sharp gasps. But the barrel of the revolver was levelled steadily at the head of the German.

BOOK III

Chapter Twenty-Three

Bumpkin: that was what barrister Kenneth P. Linstrom was thinking about as he drove towards a court appearance in Ocho Rio. And it was no wonder. He worked with bumpkin, played with bumpkin, got grind from bumpkin, drank rum with bumpkin, and was constantly at loggerheads with bumpkin. As far as the barrister was concerned, bumpkin grew on tree in Jamaica, and any man who lived here was chucked higgledy-piggledy into the middle of bumpkin mentality. In his view the motto written under the alligator on the country's coat of arms should be, "Out of Many, One Bumpkin." Anything else there was a damn lie.

The barrister was a brown skinned man with greying hair so impeccably distinguished and well-placed on his temples that it looked as if he had painted it there for theatrical effect. The barrister had it all: brawn, brain, good looks, five children, big house, Mercedes Benz, sailboat, and a successful law practice. On top of everything else, he played a ferocious game of weekend cricket.

During his desultory thinking about bumpkin, Linstrom was driving through the highlands of St. Ann whose lush scenery spoke of constant rain, fog, and morning dew. He was on his way to the small courthouse in Ocho Rios to defend good against evil, mercy against malice, principle against bumpkin. He was appearing at his own cost in the defence of Aloysius, who was being tried along with Inga and Service on the charge of burglary and attempted murder.

This involvement of Barrister Linstrom in this insignificant country case was typical of his quixotic nature. He had merely happened one morning to read about an upcoming trial in which a madman, a butcher, and a German woman were being tried for breaking and entering, felonious assault and attempted murder of a St. Ann landowner. But what had caught his attention was the report that the landowner's life had been saved by the lunatic. The story was garbled with the usual journalistic porridge, but the barrister was nevertheless struck by its obvious assemblage of good and evil.

He was sitting on the veranda of his Beverly Hills house when he first read the story. Spread out below the terrace on which he had eaten breakfast was a panoramic vista of Kingston complete with morning haze, Palisadoes peninsular, clogged lines of traffic, and in the distance, the sleek blue of the Caribbean. Affluence, prosperity, and bumpkin mansions surrounded the barrister on all sides but did not seduce him. No matter that a swimming pool lay a few feet from his toes, a Mercedes Benz was parked a little distance behind his neckback, and four maids were bustling his children off to school inside the house just beyond his right ear, in his heart he was still a devout socialist.

Of course, bumpkin found the barrister's socialism hypocritical and perplexing. Bumpkin thought in black and white and always got vexed when a socialist didn't live in a hovel and wear rags on his back. But ask bumpkin about heaven and listen to what he said. Ask him if he was praying to go to heaven so he could eat thin gruel and day-old soup and sleep in a stinking hovel with a leaky roof like he expected socialists to do, and he would laugh in your face. Bumpkin heaven meant fat roast beef, rice and peas and all the yellow yam you could eat. Ask pumpkin and he would tell you that angels didn't live in ramshackle house and ride on donkey cart. Angel house was high on a hill with a view and a breeze, had chandeliers, swimming pool and marble staircase. Maybe even a demon maid or two from the country who would fix you a cup of tea in the morning and scratch you foot bottom at night. If wealth was good enough for heaven and angels, it was good enough for socialism and socialists.

That very morning, Barrister Linstrom had rung up the country counsel assigned to defend Aloysius and offered his services. The man was taken aback – he knew of course the name of Linstrom by reputation – and stammered that he had merely intended to advise his client to plead guilty and throw himself at the mercy of the court. Fuzzy thinking, Linstrom had retorted sternly. What about the man's alleged madness, what about the act of mercy he had shown by preventing a murder? Well, replied the attorney, the man was mad and if he didn't end up in jail he'd probably wind up in the asylum. As far as he could tell it was a choice between Hee Haw and Haw Hee and wasn't worth fussing about.

Linstrom let the man have a taste of his temper. He clouted him over the phone with principle until the fellow finally told him in a surly voice that if the barrister wished to take over the case he would be more than happy to relinquish control to him. Linstrom promptly accepted and a week later drove out to Ocho Rios to meet with Aloysius.

He had a philanthropic streak in him, did this barrister. Plus he especially loved cases that gave him a chance to provoke bumpkin and unsettle bumpkin thinking.

Linstrom had two interviews with Aloysius in the dirty dark meeting room of the jailhouse. The first interview went badly because the bar next door was playing reggae music at a blaring volume and the barrister and Aloysius had to practically shout questions and answers back and forth of a soiled wooden table.

The second interview took place on a Sunday when the raucousness of the bar was subdued and the only background noise was a moan of hymns from several village churches. This time the barrister went over Aloysius's involvement in the robbery, learned some scant details about the German woman who had talked him into taking part in it, and discovered the man named Service who had struck a blow wounding the landowner had since become a repentant Seventh Day Adventist and intended to throw himself on the mercy of the court.

The barrister summed up his view of the case to Aloysius.

"You have one main problem," he said. "I'll give it to you in a word: bumpkin."

Aloysius blinked.

"Bumpkin, sah?"

"Yes. That is your problem. I could put it another way but basically it boil down to that. You going to have a bumpkin judge, bumpkin jury, and worst of all, bumpkin mentality to cope with. But the one good thing you have on your side is that you have a barrister who love to fight bumpkin. I going to get you off if it's the last thing I do."

"What name, 'bumpkin', sah?" Aloysius asked timidly.

"Let me put it this way. Bumpkin is my name for a certain way of thinking we find all over Jamaica from top to bottom. It's like a gas in de air."

Aloysius grinned.

"You know, sah, when me was a little boy me auntie used to say dat me have a mind like a barrister."

"Is dat so?"

The barrister gathered his notes and stuffed them into his briefcase.

"But me auntie dead when me was a little boy and me never learned to read and write."

"Just as well. Too much damn barrister already in this country."

"But I wonder, sah. Could you tell me how it feel to be a famous barrister?"

Linstrom peered hard into the loamy eyes of the madman searching his face in the dim room.

"Being a barrister in Jamaica mean you have bumpkin round you neck from de time you get up in de morning to de time you go to sleep at night. That's the God's truth about being a barrister. Bumpkin make you fart grease and shit fire."

When Linstrom got to the tiny courthouse in Ocho Rios many of the players in the morality drama – or so he had described the case to his associates in law and socialism – were already there. The German woman was sitting at a table with two burly policewomen standing behind her. Her Jamaican barrister and her father sat with her along with another white man identified to the court as the family's personal lawyer brought over from Germany to observe the proceedings. The three white people wore a thin smile that reminded the barrister of a mouth whose corners had been slit open with a sharp razor.

Inga's father was impeccably dressed in a blue suit appropriate for the grey climate of the north and suggestive of custom tailoring. He wore a stern expression and started at every sound as though he were expecting at any moment to witness some bizarre event he had been steeling himself to face. Linstrom instinctively disliked him. To the barrister nothing in the world was uglier than a rich white man. Let a white man get rich and suddenly his fingers got fat and smooth like restaurant shrimp, his head and face grew shiny from endless buffing with scents and soap, and sooner or later he ended up looking like a freshly polished tooth.

The German lawyer look out a legal pad and prepared to take notes. Inga sat sullenly between the two men. When Aloysius walked into the courtroom she waved and smiled at him, drawing a grimace from the lawyer and a warning frown from her father.

Service, looking nervous and repentant, wobbled into the courtroom between two constables, sat down at the table reserved for him and his lawyer, and immediately and conspicuously opened a Bible and began reading it in a mumble.

Busha and Sarah were also present. Busha still wore a thick bandage around his arm where he had been chopped. Sarah held his uninjured hand and whispered often to him.

The jury had just been seated when Linstrom made his first move. He approached the judge and wondered aloud in a peevish voice why the white woman was being granted preferential treatment by the court. The three Germans stared at him. The judge asked him to explain what he meant.

"I just can't help wondering why these two white men are allowed to sit at the defense table. Are they employed as counsel?"

The judge squirmed.

"Complexion has nothing to do with sitting at any table," the judge remonstrated with a frown.

"But I have to ask myself if that is what makes the difference," Linstrom said loudly, facing the brown and black jury. "I mean, these white men are not on trial. This white woman is on trial."

"Why does the honorable gentleman keep bring up their complexion?" the judge asked.

"To identify them, sah. These are white people. If I was talking about a brown horse, I'd say 'brown horse' and nobody would think I mean the black one."

Inga's barrister jumped up and said that one white man was the father of the accused and the other was his personal counsel from Germany.

"Are you qualified to practice law in Jamaica, sah?" Linstrom asked the German who was identified as the lawyer.

The German smiled indignantly.

"I am accredited to the Vorld Court," he said smoothly.

"My question is whether you have been admitted to the Jamaican bar."

"I am here in an unofficial capacity at my client's request."

"So you don't mind sitting where everybody else must sit who has no business in this court, do you? I mean, you don't think that being a white man entitles you to sit in the front of the bus even though you are not driving?"

"You Honour!" Inga's barrister roared. "This gentleman is out of order!"

"Mr. Linstrom, I will repeat. Complexion has nothing to do with this case."

"You Honour," Linstrom retorted, addressing the jury, "it has everything to do with this case. My client is a poor black man who had been in and out of the madhouse all his life. He is what we call in Jamaica a 'sufferer' – one of the many among us carrying the heaviest load. The man whose house he is accused of breaking, and whose life he saved, is a white man. The wicked woman you see sitting before you there, who used sex and money to inveigle this poor black man to become a thief, is white. The third defendant, who stands accused of striking the blow, is a black man. Don't make ghost fool you that colour don't have anything to do with this case. Colour has everything to do with this case, sah. Colour and money."

The German lawyer and Inga's father stood up.

"Ve vill take our seat vith the spectators," the lawyer said to the judge.

"I would like to warn the honourable gentleman," the judge said darkly, "that I don't want any rabble-rousing in my court room."

Linstrom flashed his most engaging smile.

"Where you see rabble in this courtroom, Your Honour?" He peered around him as though searching for rabble. "I don't see a one. I see a very intelligent looking jury. But I see no rabble that anybody could want to rouse."

The jury's collective face was wreathed with a grin. Satisfied with himself, Linstrom sat down. The jury beamed in his direction.

Nothing sweeted bumpkin more than to be told they had brains. Not even pum-pum.

Chapter Twenty-Four

Busha was on the stand giving his testimony about the Sunday of the robbery and the injury he had received. Busha said he had nearly bled to death that day because it took some time to attract attention from the street and get a passer-by to go into the village and bring back the police. Until then, he just lay on the floor of his own drawing room bleeding while Sarah kept the gun trained on the three robbers.

It was one terrible thing after another on that fateful day, Busha said heavily. When he got to the hospital they had to send for the doctor in the bird bush and by the time he arrived Busha's arm had gone completely numb all the way down his fingers. In fact, Busha said, flexing his fingers, even to this day he could barely make a fist. Plus one of his fingers didn't want to close right. He held up his hand and showed where the middle finger was still stiff.

The crown counsel led Busha through the story, through the encounters he had had with the German woman, through his medical treatments in Jamaica and America, and finally, to an identification of the three robbers sitting in the courtroom.

When it was time to cross-examine, Barrister Linstrom walked over to the dock and enquired of Busha in a polite voice how he felt today.

Busha looked gloomy and said he didn't feel well at all. He hadn't felt well since the chopping.

Linstrom asked to see Busha's injured arm, touched the stiff finger and tried to get it to bend back. It curled back into its rigid position.

"Mr. McIntosh," Linstrom said sympathetically, "I want you to know that I sympathize with you. It must have been a dreadful experience to come to your own home on a peaceful Sunday, surprise three thief in your drawing room, and have one of them try to murder you."

"De doctor say it's de worst chop he ever saw in all his years of medicine," Busha said darkly. "He said de bone was almost chopped in two pieces. He said that bone was tougher than wood, tougher dan some metal. He said that when you see bone chop nearly in two, you know dat it got a good blow."

Linstrom did a turn around the small room and ended up in front of the jury box where he squinted solemnly at Busha.

"But it could have been worse, Mr. McIntosh," the barrister said. "Except that my client intervened and prevented any further injury."

Busha stared at his feet.

"Except that my client showed mercy, Mr. McIntosh," Linstrom prompted.

Busha glared at him.

"Mercy?" he growled. "Dat's what you call 'mercy'? A thief break into you house and you call dat 'mercy'? What kind of mercy is dat? A man stick out one 'o you eye and leave de odder one and dat's mercy? Is dat what you call mercy?"

"Not the same man, Mr. McIntosh," Linstrom said smoothly, glancing at the jury. "Don't forget that one man struck the blow whereas the other man, my client over there, showed the mercy."

Busha glowered.

"He broke into my house! He was the one dat locked up de dogs in the garage! De dogs know him because he used to work for me! Dat's what you call mercy?"

"Just a minute, Mr. McIntosh. Fair is fair. Now I grant you that my client should not have broken into your house. However, I understand the reasoning that led him to do it … ."

"Reasoning?" Busha cried indignantly. "The man is a madman! Which madman you know have reasoning? They should've locked him up ten years ago and throw away de damn key!"

Linstrom walked over to his desk and took up a folder stuffed with papers.

"Mr. McIntosh," he said, "let us say that for argument's sake I am a thief."

"You could be a thief for all I know," Busha grunted nastily. "I don't know you from Adam."

"Good. So now I am a thief. And I have a little brain about me. Times are hard on me and I decide to do a little thiefing. So I look around me to see who I can thief from. I spot three houses I think I can thief from. Two of them belong to poor people. One of them belong to a rich man. Which house you think I would thief, if I was a thief?"

"What does this line of questioning have to do with this case, Your Honour?" the crown counsel asked impatiently.

Busha got red in the face.

"So you saying dat because I might have a nice house a man can come and nearly murder me on a Sunday afternoon? You saying dat it's my fault dat dese three wretches break into me house and nearly kill me?"

"Of course it is not your fault, Mr. McIntosh.," Linstrom assured him. "I just showing you that although I don't agree with what my client did, he did it for a reason. There was method in his madness. In fact, the only mad thing he did that day was to show mercy. Admit it, Mr. McIntosh, that if Aloysius hadn't done that mad thing of showing you mercy you wouldn't be here today complaining about chopping."

Busha stamped his feet angrily.

"Listen me, Mr. Linstrom. I was born in dis parish in de same house I live in today. My grand-daddy built dat house, not me! My great-great-great grand-daddy buy dat land dat I farm and raise cow on today. I didn't buy it. Not one square inch! I was born into it. Did I ask to be born into it? Did I ask even be born? I don't take nothing from anybody. I never trouble anybody! Dese damn people break me house and nearly kill me in me own drawing room on a Sunday, and why? Because it's my fault to be born! Dat's reason enough to kill a man? And look at what dey do to me? Look at my finger!"

Busha waved his stiff finger over his head for everyone to see.

"What I do to deserve this? According to this man, I was born with a little property, and so I deserve to get chopped! If I'd known it would come to dis so help me God when I was coming out of me mother womb I'd have hung on for dear life and stay dere in de dark rather dan be born on dis damn island and be chopped."

"Mr. McIntosh," Linstrom pressed in an aggrieved tone, "Didn't my client show you mercy? Didn't he save your life?"

"MERCY!" Busha roared. "DIS IS MERCY?"

He stabbed his stiff finger like an icepick accusingly in the direction of the barrister.

Linstrom said he had no further questions.

Sarah testified the following day. Busha did not appear with her at the courthouse. She told her story calmly to the jury, explaining that she had fired a single shot with her husband's pistol at one of the men she identified as Service because he was standing over her wounded husband and about to kill him with the machete. Service kept his eyes downcast during her testimony.

Inga's barrister asked whether or not Sarah had seen Inga strike her husband. Sarah replied that she had not but that Inga had pulled Aloysius off Service, who had then been able to get the machete. Under persistent questioning, however, she had to grudgingly admit that Inga had not harmed her husband.

"Mrs. McIntosh," Linstrom asked Sarah, "did my client show your husband mercy?"

Sarah squirmed.

"Mr. Linstrom, I wish you wouldn't put it that way. That's what upset Hubert. You make it sound as though Aloysius was innocent when in fact he was there to thief from us."

"But, Mrs. McIntosh," Linstrom insisted, "isn't it a fact that he saved your husband's life?"

Sarah groped visibly for words.

"He jumped on that one there," she said, pointing to Service, "who had chopped Hubert and was going to chop him again. While they were fighting I was able to run into the bedroom and get the gun."

"So, in fact, it was his act of mercy that saved your husband's life?"

"Mr. Linstrom, I'm not as smart as you are about these things. Aloysius had a change of heart, but 'mercy' just seems to me to be the wrong word for what he did."

"Why, ma'am? Explain that to me."

"Because when I think of mercy I think of goodness, softheartedness, kindness. I don't think of a thief breaking into an innocent man's house and stopping an accomplice from killing him."

"But wasn't it a kindness of my client to spare your husband's life, Mrs. McIntosh?"

Sarah looked weary.

"I suppose so."

"And wasn't it an act of mercy?"

"If it was mercy, God spare us more of it," she said with feeling.

Service gave his testimony the following day. Before he even got to the witness box and was sworn in, he broke down and began a soulful sobbing. His defense counsel led him through a tearful recital of how he had come to St. Ann seeking butchering work and had fallen in with the German woman and her madman lover, how the woman had enticed him into lovemaking and inveigled him into breaking into the house of a white man he'd only seen a few times in the district. He sobbed that he hadn't meant to injure anyone and that he'd struck the blow because he was fearful that Busha had a gun and would shoot him.

His testimony brought an occasional tittering or clucking from the spectators and the jury. He described how Inga had held him down and used him for sex, how she had made them build a small house in the bush, how she had established what she said was the rule of "pum-pum."

The judge could not believe his ears and made him repeat the nasty phrase, "rule of pum-pum" two times before it finally sank in.

"You mean to tell me," the judge asked with obvious disbelief, "that a woman could hold down a big man like you against his will?"

"Yes, sah!" Service cried indignantly. "She hold me down, sah! She know kung-fu and chop suey and marital arts, sah!"

"Marital arts? Chop suey?" the judge scoffed. "What you talking 'bout man? One is when a man marry and de odder is Chinese food."

"Me no know what name you call it, sah," Service bawled pitifully, "all me know is dat she strong, sah! She break up any man in dis room. She chop off tree limb wid her bare hands, sah! She strong, sah! Two man can't beat dat woman."

Unimpressed, the judge grunted and waved at him to continue.

Service described the furious bouts of lovemaking with him and Aloysius alternating as her partners and tearfully babbled about how her gluttonous appetite for men wore both of them down so that neither one of them could walk straight and yet she would still want more. He paused frequently to sob loudly or to wipe his eyes and blow his nose.

During his testimony Inga's father sat up erect in his chair staring grimly ahead, his hands clenched tightly in his lap. He looked like an animal rigidly frozen in the presence of a predator. The German lawyer took a steady stream of notes. Inga yawned, slouched, doodled and occasionally gazed around the room.

When he had finished with the story, Service talked about his imprisonment and how a kindhearted warden had lent him a bible to read and had made him see that he was a wicked sinner and badly needed to change his ways before Judgement Day.

At the end of his testimony, Service begged forgiveness of Busha, who was not in the courtroom, and of Sarah who was and stared at him with contempt. He pleaded with the court to have mercy on him and remember that he was still a young man with his whole life ahead.

Linstrom approached for cross-examination.

"So you get religion in de jailhouse?" Linstrom asked familiarly.

"Yes, sah."

"What about mud, now?"

"Mud, sah? Me don't understand, sah."

"You not de man who used to say dat mud was God to you, dat mud do dis, dat and de odder. You not de man who used to say dat mud is supreme over all things?"

"Me, sah? Me say dat, sah? No, sah! Mud, sah! How anybody can say dat 'bout mud?"

Linstrom paced near the witness-box, peering scornfully at him.

"I going to ask you one question. What stop you from killing Busha McInstosh?"

Service hung his head.

"Me get a shot, sah," he said faintly.

Linstrom turned and practically spat in his face.

"You damn liar, you! Aloysius didn't grab you and stop you from chopping Mr. McIntosh?"

Service looked as though his feelings were hurt.

"Grab me, sah? How do you mean, 'grab me'?"

"Grab you, you damn brute! Grab you and prevent you from murdering de man who was fluttering on de floor!"

"Me fall down, sah! When me got up de woman shot me!"

"Vhat liar you are!" Inga shouted. "Tell the truth!"

"Is you do dis to me!" Service shrieked, pointing a quivering finger at her. "Is you bring me to dis! Is you mad up me brain wid pum-pum and make dem put me in de workhouse! Is your fault dis!"

The judge pounded his gavel.

"You're out of order!"

Service sobbed wildly.

"Is she bring me to dis, sah! She mad up me brain wid pum-pum and do dis to me!"

He was reduced to moaning and blubbering uncontrollably.

"Idiot!" Inga's voice rang loud with contempt.

Like some hydra-headed monster, the jury turned as one and peered silently at her.

The next day she was gone. The story broke in the *Star* with a smudgy splash of headlines: the German woman had simply walked out of the jail. Bribery of the guards was suspected. Even though her passport had been seized, she was believed to have been whisked off the island by her father and his attorney, both of whom had also disappeared.

"Good riddance!" the crown counsel was unofficially quoted as having said about her disappearance.

The remark was bitterly denied by a spokesperson who declared that come what may the government intended to apply to the Republic of West Germany for the extradition of the fugitive Inga Schmidt.

But that was very plainly that.

Chapter Twenty-Five

Barrister Linstrom put Aloysius on the stand to give testimony. It was expected to be the final day of the case. Busha and Sarah were in court to witness its outcome, and Aloysius glanced nervously at them during his testimony.

The barrister began by saying that he just wanted the jury to hear for themselves his client's side of the story. He also wanted the jury to get to know his client a little better and to appreciate the part he'd played in this sad business.

By now the jury was thoroughly disgusted and was longing to go away from the cramped and stuffy courtroom where the overhead fan didn't work and the windows were left half closed to shut out the noise of the street and everything was so airless and drab that even drawing breath was hard work.

Sensing the jury's impatience, the barrister got down quickly to brass tacks. He asked Aloysius a few questions about life with Inga and then led him quickly to matters that struck every observer as stupidly irrelevant.

"Lemme ask you dis, Aloysius," the barrister said, standing right beside the jury. "If I ask you for a character reference, whose name would you give me?"

Aloysius shuffled his feet and looked pained.

"I don't know, sah."

"Who is you best friend in de whole world? Who know you as man better dan anybody else in de world?"

Aloysius fidgeted.

"De tree, sah," he said faintly.

"What's dat, Aloysius?" the barrister prompted.

Aloysius took a deep breath.

"De tree, sah. De flame heart tree. Him know me best of everybody."

The jury sniggered at this idiotic reply, causing Aloysius to shuffle and look embarrassed.

"Now, Aloysius," the barrister said gently, "you know what people going to say to dat. Dey goin' say dat a tree can't talk."

"So dey say, sah," Aloysius mumbled, looking mystified.

"So what did de tree say 'bout dis German woman, now?"

"Him didn't like her, sah. Him was jealous."

"Speak up, man," Linstrom prompted. "Dey can't hear you."

"Him didn't like her, sah. Him was jealous."

"Him didn't like her, eh? Why him didn't like her?"

Aloysius shot an apprehensive glance at the jury.

"Because before she come, it was just him and me. But then when she come de three of us was dere, and him get jealous."

"Him tell you dis himself?"

Aloysius squirmed.

"Yes, sah."

"So if I ask you for somebody to give me a reference about you in writing, you'd pick dis tree?"

"Yes, sah. Except dat him can't write."

The jury guffawed.

"But me can't write neither, sah," Aloysius added in a soft voice. "Odderwise everybody used to say dat me'd be a barrister."

"Oh, yes? Well, lemme ask you now, Aloysius. How did you feel about this woman?"

Aloysius hung his head.

"Me love Inga, sah."

"Love!" the barrister said, nodding his head. "Everybody in dis room understand love. But I goin' tell you what nobody here understand. Nobody understand why you jump in and spare Mr. McIntosh's life. Why did you do dat, Aloysius?"

Aloysius rubbed his face and sighed.

"Me feel sorry for him, sah," he said softly.

In the back of the courtroom Busha jumped angrily to his feet.

"Feel sorry for me? You feel sorry for me, you mad rass you! You broke into me house and nearly make a man kill me and you have de nerve to say dat you feel sorry for me?"

"Out of order, Busha!" the judge bellowed, banging his gavel.

"Him is out of order saying dat him feel sorry for me! Damn nerve!" Bush fumed, sitting back down. Sarah patted his arm and whispered in his ear.

Linstrom looked from Busha to Aloysius and then to the jury.

"So de tree is you best friend, eh? You love de tree?"

"Yes, sah," Aloysius mumbled, looking ashamed to admit it.

"And you love Inga?"

"Yes, sah. Inga is me true love."

"And you feel sorry for Mr. McIntosh?"

"Yes, sah. When me see him get de chop."

"So in a way, you could say dat you love Busha McIntosh, too?"

"LOVE ME!" Busha roared, leaping again to his feet. "LOVE YOU, RASS! LOVE WHO?"

"Busha!" the judge shouted.

Sarah grabbed Busha by the elbow and propelled him firmly out the back door.

"What kind of madhouse is dis dat turn thiefing into loving?" Busha yelled over his shoulder as he whisked through the doorway.

When everyone had quietened down, the barrister strolled slowly over to his table.

"One final question," he said. "Aloysius, what is your name?"

Aloysius looked startled.

"Name, sah? What me name?"

"Yes. Tell me your full name."

"Me name, sah? Me full, full name?"

"Yes. What is your name?"

Aloysius struggled visibly with himself in the witness stand. Then he straightened up briskly.

"Aloysius Gossamer Longshoreman Technocracy Predominate Involuted Enraptured Parliamentarian Patriarch Verdure Emulative ..."

The jury looked stunned. The judge repeatedly banged his gavel. Linstrom began putting away his papers in a briefcase.

"Perihelion Dichotomy Intellectual Chaste Iron-Curtain Linkage Colonialistic Dilapidated ...

"Order!" the judge banged. "Order in the court!"

"Impracticable Loquacious Predilection ...

Two constables led Aloysius bodily away. He continued his rapid-fire recital as he was manhandled out the door.

"Abomination   Vichyssoise   Pyrrhic   Mountebank Unconscionable Altercation Lookalike ...

"Go 'way you mad rass you!" Busha was heard bellowing at him from behind the courthouse.

Bumpkin loved a show as much as bumpkin loved money, and the barrister gave them a show with his summation and closing

argument. It was dreadfully hot in the courtroom and the two
rows of black and brown faces before the pacing barrister were
gleaming with sweat. Handkerchiefs fluttered in the room
mopping brows and wiping sweaty nosebridges and every now
and again one of the jurors, an old man who said he was a
retired teacher, would gulp for breath like a fish out of water.

Busha sat fuming in the back of the room listening to the
barrister's speech and getting redder and redder in the face.
Once or twice Busha even snorted with contempt and drew a
glare of reproof from the judge, who was his personal friend and
did not want to be too hard on him.

The barrister began his summation by telling the jury that
he wanted them to understand why he did not live in America.
To give them this understanding, he rolled up his sleeves,
leaned his arms on the railing of the jury box, and begged the
jurors to look closely at the colour of his skin.

Carrying on like a schoolteacher, he asked each one of them
what colour his skin was. The answers, given after careful study
and hesitation, ranged from light brown to khaki to chestnut.
The barrister then paced around the room, lowered his voice
and said he would tell everyone present his secret about why he
didn't live in America even though a man like himself in
America would live in a mansion, drive big car, earn bands of
money and go through his whole life without ever laying eyes
on a madman.

"But I don't live in America," the barrister said, "because in
America dey would say I am a black man."

He paused for this sad state of affairs to sink into the twin
tiers of bumpkin stacked attentively before him.

"Now everyone here see dat I am a brown man except the
American. To him, I am a black man. To the American a brown
man, a red man, a sepia man, a chestnut man, a khaki man, is

one and de same: him is a black man. But notice dis about Americans. Dey don't call brown horse black. Dey don't call brown dog black. Dey don't call brown house black. Is only brown man dey call black. Because over dere dey have more colour for horse and house and dog dan dey have for man. For a man dey have only two colour: white and black."

The barrister did a little spin around the room and wound up face to face with bumpkin row.

"But here in Jamaica we have our brown man, our dark brown man, our yellow man, our red man, our pink man – dat is you Chiny man – our Indian man, and our blueblack man! Because we don't see a man only in two colour in Jamaica because God don't make man in only two colour. God make man in at least thirty forty colour, and here in Jamaica we see dem all."

Busha snorted like a horse blowing its nose.

"So now," continue the barrister, "it's like dis man, Aloysius Hobson, who say him have a thousand names. You are Jamaicans and you can look at him and see dat him is not just a thief."

"Him is a damn thief, of course!" Busha snapped, drawing a rap of the gavel.

"You can see him did a little thiefing and him is a little mad, and him is a little fool-fool. But you also see dat dis heart have some good in it too. Dat dis is de same heart dat show mercy to Busha McIntosh, dat when push come to shove would not let dis damn wretch here who say him is born-again Christian kill Busha – born again me backfoot! Him born again like monkey born again when monkey want something from you! – you can see dat love live in dis poor heart beside thiefing and foolishness and madness, love and mercy also live dere side by side."

"Love for who?" Busha snorted.

"Love for you, sah!" the barrister trumpeted, turning to face Busha who glowered in the back of the room. "Dis is a man who love you! Who show mercy to you! Every breath of life you draw from now on until you day of judgement you going owe to dis madman here!"

"Owe what?" Busha raged, jumping to his feet. "So what, him is God over me now? Him make me?"

"Make you, sah?" Linstrom declared. "Yes, sah. Look on dis poor madman before you. Because now on until you dead, dis man is you maker!"

Busha's face turned purple and full like an overripe grape.

"My God not black!" Busha screamed. "Maybe your God black, but my God not black! My God in heaven, him don't talk to tree and him don't thief from people house!"

"Busha!" the judge yelled, rapping the gavel.

Still yelling about his God, Busha was escorted out of the room by two bemused constables.

Linstrom watched him go with a sly grin on his face.

Then he turned to the bumpkins who were fanning themselves and mopping their faces before him.

"If you convict dis man today," he said to them in a hushed voice, "it mean one thing. You turn American on me. It mean you overlook de mercy and love dat's in dis man's heart. It mean you call brown man, sepia man, red man, and yellow man black. It mean you see more in dog and horse and rat and cat dan you see in a man. It mean all you see in dis heart is thiefing and wickedness, but you don't see de kindness and mercy and love dat live dere too."

The barrister sat down, signalling that his speech was done.

"Is all right, sah," Service mumbled in a pitiful voice. "Me forgive you for saying wicked thing 'bout me. De Lord say to forgive, and me forgive you."

"I don't hold discourse with born thief and bogus Christian," Listrom said sternly.

"Me forgive you for dat too," Service cringed, pawing the Bible with moist fingers.

The jury was out for a matter of only minutes and came back with a decision. It was so insufferably hot in the deliberation room that debate was nearly impossible. But none was really necessary because the jurors were all of the same opinion on the principles in the case. They found Service guilty, Aloysius innocent.

The barrister smiled when the verdict was read. Aloysius, standing to hear it, shuffled his feet and looked confused.

"Me guilty and him innocent!" Service bawled loudly. "How dat? Him no broke de house wid me too? Is me alone broke it? How me de only one going to workhouse for it, when is three of us broke de house?

His counsel nudged him in the ribs.

"Is all right," Service mumbled in a suddenly subdued voice. "Dey crucified de Lord and Saviour, so I suppose dem must crucify me too."

On being informed of the verdict, Busha gave a roar of outrage so loud that it blew from the parking lot into the courtroom, scaring a woman in the front row out of her wits and causing her to jump as if she'd sat on a pin.

"Mercy must be shown where mercy is shown," the old juror was explaining in a pedantic voice as he shuffled out of the courtroom with the other members.

"Rass, boy," said one the jurors, "lemme outta dis damn madhouse. It hotter dan hellfire in dere."

The judge sentenced Service to fifteen years at hard labour. Then he said that in good conscience he would not allow a madman who had participated in a burglary to get away scot free, so he was sending Aloysius back to the lunatic asylum for further treatment.

Aloysius was sent to Kingston, spent a month in the asylum, was subjected to experimental American treatment based on diet rich in protein, administered a few pills, beaten once with a switch, and released as harmless.

The building guard who walked Aloysius to the gate, and who had become rather fond of him, remarked to the gatepost guard as they watched him walk away to the bus stop:

"Any man in Jamaica who can chat to a bush and tree will never be lonely. Sometimes, to rass, me wish me could chat wid bush, too."

"Man who chat wid bush can't become civil servant," the gatepost guard said scornfully, turning the pages of his book.

He was studying to become a clerk in a government ministry and rightly suspected that talking to bushes and trees was not the kind of madness appreciated in such high places.

Chapter Twenty-Six

The widow Dawkins, the same who had nearly asphyxiated Busha with her beastly farting in church, did not like nastiness to touch her lips. She did not like bad words to cross her tongue or filthy expressions to brush against her teeth whether real or false (she had both kinds in her mouth).

So when Aloysius asked her to read his foreign letter – the one he had lately got from the slack German who had talked him into breaking Busha's house and nearly made him party to murder – she made it plain that if there were any bad words in it she would not utter them but would simply signify their omission by saying "nastiness" or "filthiness."

Aloysius agreed. They were sitting on the small wooden veranda of the widow's house, which was half encircled by a grove of trees on a mountain slope overlooking the endless stretches of Busha's land. It was dusk and the sky bled the soft pastel colours of a tropical sunset.

The widow was perched on her rocking chair, the same she had been sitting in when her faithful departed husband had dropped dead of a heart attack four years ago. She had on her thick glasses and clutched the letter Aloysius had been told was waiting for him at the Post Office and had now brought to her for reading.

She steeled herself with a deep breath and began:

"Dear Aloysius, I am writing from Rome, where I have enlisted in a cell of the Red Brigade. You might not have heard of the Red Brigade in Jamaica, but we are a political group fighting for the rights of poor people here and everywhere else in the world. At the moment I am living in the basement of a house in a suburb of Rome. I do not go out very much because the police are everywhere looking for us.

"I think of you often. Most often of all, I think of … nastiness, filthiness … Do you remember the days when we used to … more nastiness, more filthiness."

The widow turned the page, glanced at Aloysius and muttered grimly,

"A whole page of filthiness."

She dismissed a paragraph on the next page with, "A paragraph of nastiness."

Finally she found a clean passage and began reading again.

"My father tried to have me committed to an institution in Berne, which is in Switzerland. I pretended that I would go and to accept his decision. But I managed to escape the two men he had hired to take me there. Since then I have been living in Italy with friends.

"I am sorry that everything turned so bad for you. I am also sorry that Service was such … nastiness and filthiness. I do not know even to this day why I let him come and live with us because he was … nastiness and filthiness."

The widow paused and drew a cleansing breath.

Aloysius fidgeted and peered over her shoulder at the words scrawled on the page and wished with all his heart that he himself could read them and see what lay under the "nastiness and filthiness" that gave the widow such discomfort.

"I do not know if I will ever again come to Jamaica," the widow read.

"I sincerely hope not," she sniffed.

"In fact, I do not know how my life will turn out and how it might end. That stupid old man who controls us all …"

"What old man does she mean?" the widow wondered.

Aloysius squirmed.

"God."

"God? She calling 'God Almighty' a stupid old man? You sure is God she mean?"

"Yes, ma'am. Dat what she call God."

"But what a nerve of dis dirty woman," the widow declared angrily, "to write dat way about God!"

"Beg you finish de letter for me, ma'am."

"You not going catch me talking about God in dat way. No sirreehheee. Not dis woman."

"Just pass over dat part, please."

"I only doing dis because is you, Aloysius," the widow said piously. "No man going make dis woman commit sin."

"Me not making you commit sin, Ma'am."

"In fact, I do not know how my life will turn out and how it might end. Nastiness … who controls us all will no doubt have some tricks in store for this sheep. But I still show him my teeth in the pasture."

"Teeth? Show who teeth? What she mean by dat?"

Aloysius said he did not quite know.

"Thank God, it soon done!" the widow breathed, scanning the letter.

She continued reading.

"Aloysius, remember me. I have not forgotten … nastiness and filthiness and more nastiness … And I hope to see you again one day either in this life or in the next one."

"What next life?" the widow asked, handing Aloysius the letter with a visible sigh of relief.

Aloysius took the letter, ran his fingers gently over it, folded it up carefully and tucked it in his shirt pocket.

"Inga believe she live before and she goin' live again," he muttered.

"That is not what scripture say," the widow said firmly. "She believe in what dey call 'reincarnation', but scripture don't say nothing about dat. Reincarnation is foolishness."

"Yes, Ma'am."

The widow leaned back on her rocker and gave it a brisk ride. The floorboards creaked and the endless acres of Busha's land spread out below the railings of her veranda seemed to her to bounce up and down like a stormy ocean.

Since Aloysius had been released from the asylum, the widow had taken him firmly in hand. Their friendship had begun quite unexpectedly. The widow had been taking a shortcut across an open pasture, a thing she did only if she was late for evening service (from childhood she had been terrified and distrustful of cows). As bad luck would have it she ran smack into a herd of grazing cattle. A calf began running friskily around her, pawing the ground, and the beast even lowered its head as if to charge and buck her with its nubby horns. She tried to shoo it away with her umbrella, which did no good, so she stopped in her tracks and let loose a piercing scream.

Aloysius came running from the small house under the flame heart tree, drove off the playful calf, and escorted the widow to the road, even helping her climb over the cut-stone wall. She was immediately grateful, remembered that he was a repentant sinner who had spared Busha's life, and invited him that very evening to come to her house after service and take dinner with her.

That was more than three months ago. A relationship had developed quickly between them since then, which led eventually to Aloysius moving into the back room of the widow's house, doing some little yard work around the garden for her, and getting in exchange good hot meals, companionship, and daily management.

The relationship between the two of them was ruled entirely by the widow. She knew from experience that man without woman was prone to vagabond behaviour, dissolute living, and assorted wickedness. Management was what men needed – management by a strong woman. In God's plan, man was a shop and woman the shopkeeper. Ever since the death of her husband, the widow had been an unemployed keeper in search of a shop. She had been lonely and depressed. Her days had been spent in dreary solitude; some nights she could only cry herself to sleep. Her only daughter had risen high in the world and gone off to live and bear children in foreign places. Men were scarce. Those who could walk and talk already had a string of women. The few unattached ones were at death's door.

Yet the widow was not yet ready for the graveyard. She was only four years older than Aloysius, strong and healthy in mind and body, and bent on living another thirty years. That is, of course, if she could find a man. For the widow was no fool. She well understood the ways of womanly flesh. No matter what parson might say, without a man to air her out every now and again and prevent her vital passages from clogging like old pipe, a woman could easily drop dead in her prime.

So three weeks after she assured management of Aloysius, after she had made him take regular baths, fed him several hot meals, given him fresh sheets to sleep on, read him passages nightly from the Bible, the widow lured him one rainy night into her bedroom and got a good and healthful cleaning out in the pitch darkness.

The next morning she drew the sweetest breath since the days of her childhood. An annoying pimple on her nose began drying up. When she walked down the hillside to tend to her callaloo garden, she bounded over rockstone and gravel like goat kid. The whole day long she hoed and cleaned out garden beds, singing hymns all the while like she was at a revival.

Of course, there were problems with Aloysius, but nothing that couldn't be overcome by management. For one, the widow insisted that he never hold stupid conversations with bush and tree and rockstone and dog and lizard in her company. She made it plainly understood that if they were walking arm in arm on their way to church he was to make no reply to any bush or tree that should shout at him. The simple rule she asked Aloysius to live by in her presence was this: if it don't have mouth to chat wid, you can't chat wid it. If he wished to visit his favourite tree and chat with it, that was his business. He was free to come and go and chat with anything he pleased so long as she was not present.

Then there was the matter of his ignorance, which the widow could not abide. In her book, it was a sin for a God-given mind to be shut off in the darkness of illiteracy. She therefore began teaching Aloysius to read. She planned to give him lessons in Handwriting, Geography, Arithmetic, English language, and Scripture. When she was done with him, he would be able to read the *Gleaner* and the Bible. To this end she held lessons every morning on the veranda overlooking the vast reaches of Busha's pastures. Already he had learned his alphabet.

One day during a lesson the widow made the mistake of asking Aloysius his full name and he began his usual demented recital. At first she thought he was joking but when he continued to determinedly rattle off any number of stupid names, she cut him short at "Parliamentarian," with the fierce command of, "Stop dis foolishness!" in such a tone that he gasped and stopped.

He leapt to his feet, held his throat, and stammered, "Excuse me, ma'am! Me have to go to de toilet!" and ran into the toilet where he could bend over and gasp out, "Patriarch Verdure Emulative Perihelion …" and all the rest of his thousand names.

When he came out of the toilet a half-hour later the widow had made tea and was calmly preparing a lesson on diphthongs.

Busha could not get over it. The wretch who used to work for him, had broken into his house and locked up his dogs, had nearly caused him to be killed in his own drawing room, was within a matter of months walking around free and clear through the village like he paid taxes. Not only that, but the brute had also been adopted by the farting widow Dawkins with whom he consorted openly in the streets. Granted that the widow had cleaned up Aloysius, made him wear fresh clothes every day and put shoes on his feet, he was still a damn lunatic as far as Busha was concerned. You don't change mongoose nature by dressing him up like puss.

In the first few weeks after the trial, Busha's bitterness had reached a vengeful pitch. He had importuned the crown counsel to appeal, had written letters to the Bellevue Hospital warning them against releasing Aloysius, and had even considered a lawsuit against Barrister Linstrom for his part in helping a dangerous criminal escape just punishment. (Busha finally gave this idea up when his own law firm refused to hear anymore of it.)

Busha raised such a fuss that one day Barrister Linstrom went to the asylum to see how Aloysius was being treated. He was allowed to walk with the lunatic a few feet around a scrubby garden that was being tended by a uniformed inmate carrying on a conversation with his dead mother.

The barrister warned Aloysius to watch out for Busha, for there was no telling what he might do for revenge.

"Busha not going trouble me, sah," Aloysius said.

The barrister didn't agree.

"I'm telling you he's raising a fuss. He even talked about suing me."

"No, sah. Busha won't sue you."

They strolled for a moment or two in silence half-listening to the inmate gardener's chat with his dead mother.

"You know, sometimes I believe dat de worse thing you ever did," the barrister said in disgust, "is to spare dat dam white man's bumpkin life. Look where it got you! Look how it make him behave! You spare him life you lose you freedom, you girlfriend, every little thing you had. And for what? So de damn ungrateful wretch can carry on a campaign to keep you locked up in dis place for de rest of your life?"

Aloysius chuckled.

"Busha just vex, sah. Him soon feel better."

"Tell me something, Aloysius," Linstrom stopped walking and peered at the madman at his side. "Why you spare his life, eh? What was it, just a spur-of-the-moment thing?"

Aloysius looked confused at this question.

"Busha is me friend, sah. Me couldn't stand and see dem kill him so."

"You friend? Busha is your friend?"

"Yes, sah!"

"You, really mad to rass," Linstrom grunted. "Dey should lock you up in dis place for good."

"Sorry, Mumma," the mad gardener murmured. "Me never meant to mash you toe."

It got so that Busha could not endure the sight of Aloysius in the street without having a strong urge to run over the lunatic with his car. He had dreams about shooting him. Some nights he would wake up, get a gun, and sit on the veranda in the dark, hoping that he would catch the madman coming up his driveway so that he could lawfully murder him.

One night Busha went so far as to start walking down his driveway intending to go into the bushland where Aloysius lived, but he came to his senses at the gate and padded back up to his darkened house with his troop of puzzled dogs straggling after him in the moonlight.

When Aloysius became friends with the widow Dawkins and started appearing with her in church it was almost more than Busha could bear. Busha could hardly stand to be in the same parish with Aloysius much less the same church. The first time the lunatic showed up with the widow clinging to his arm, Busha stomped out of the service. After that, Busha made it a point to try to avoid any service that the widow and her new madman friend might attend.

One day Busha and Sarah brushed passed the widow and Aloysius on the church steps, and Busha muttered in a snide voice, "Is you I should be praying to. You is me God."

"Him trouble you, Busha?" the widow asked with a piercing star.

"Him nearly make dem kill me," Busha grumbled.

"Dat is in de past, Busha," the widow said firmly, putting herself between Aloysius and the white man. "He pay for dat crime and repent of dat sin. It don't become you to hold grievance, Busha. It don't become."

"Come, Hubert," Sarah urged, tugging Busha's arm.

"If you want to live wid madman dat's your business, Mrs. Dawkins," Busha growled. "But don't tell me how I must behave when I see a wretch in front of me."

"You is out of order to speak dat way to me, Busha, especially after we just come from service. Very out of order."

But all was not lost with Busha and his dream. Sarah still held firm against being buried in Kingston, but she had relented on the mausoleum. With some effort and persuasion, Busha convinced Mr. Saarem to build the mausoleum in the graveyard at Moneague. Two weeks later the construction crew descended on the dishevelled graveyard and began cleaning the foundation for a mausoleum – which the locals promptly christened a "duppy shop."

Busha lovingly supervised its building and stopped in every evening from the fields to examine the day's progress. His left arm where he had been chopped was healing well enough for him to use it to shift gearstick or even use a machete. But there was still stiffness in his middle finger, and when he talked to people he hid his injured arm behind his back so no one would have to look at it.

But with all the mausoleum Busha was still not the same man as he was before the injury. There was great bitterness in him. Some nights he could not sleep. He kept his gun under his pillow and started at the smallest sounds.

One evening he and Sarah were sitting on their veranda watching darkness fall over the pastures. Busha had seen Aloysius on the road walking with the widow Dawkins and was raging about him again.

Sarah sighed.

"You know, Hubert, sometimes I think we should leave dis place. Sometimes I think we should migrate. You just not de same man you used to be."

"Same man?" Busha glowered at her. "You expect me to be the same man after what happened?"

"You just have so much hatred in you heart for dat poor lunatic. Dat's all you talk about nowadays. De man save you life, Hubert! Why can't you accept dat and forget about it?"

"Save my life? I must accept dat he saved my life?"

"Yes. He saved your life."

"He did not save me life! You save me life by shooting dat brute! He did not save my life!"

"Hubert, he jumped on de one who was going to chop you. Because of dat I was able to get de gun. I saved you life. But he saved it too. What's the difference?"

Busha got red in the face, a sure sign that he was about to explode in anger.

"De difference is you're my wife!" Busha sputtered. "And he's a nasty old mad negar! Dat's de difference! Would you like to spend de rest of your life thinking dat every breath you drew was because of some old negar? Would you?"

Sarah sighed forbearingly.

"What's the difference? As long as I'm alive."

Busha could not endure being opposed. He meant to jump up and storm out of the house and walk off his temper in his pastures. But he didn't even make it to his feet.

Instead, he broke into a heartfelt, lonely, misunderstood sob.

Mr. Shubert was presiding over the dimly lit interior of his shop where a number of villagers were chatting the evening idly away. Through the window of the shop Mr. Shubert could see the stark white walls of Busha's duppy shop rising in the graveyard. There was a ghastly hush to the shell, and Mr. Shubert was struck by the horror and vanity implied in a man building his own tomb. It wasn't enough that one day every Jack man and woman in the world had to die, Mr. Shubert thought with a shudder, some few stupid men had to carry on about it like it was an ocean voyage.

The villagers had been making fun of Busha's duppy shop and from that the chat had turned to the change in Busha since his injury. Remarks were made about his bitterness, anecdotes were told about his sudden short-temperedness, his meanness.

Mr. Shubert was sitting behind the counter on a stool poring over his exercise book. As proprietor of the establishment, he did not often mingle in the conversations of his customers, preferring to hold himself aloof from the throng that trekked daily through his shop. But this one time he had a sudden insight he wanted to share, and he cut sharply in on a long-winded story being told by a slightly drunken cultivator named Bishop ($79.78 down in the book).

"The trouble wid Busha," Mr. Shubert said, raising his head, "Is dat him don't know God blessing when him see it. It's like Shakespeare say in dat schoolboy poem:

De quality of mercy is not strained,

It droppeth as the gentle rain from heaven,

Upon de place beneath. It is twice bless'd:

It blesseth him dat gives and him dat take.

We all owe life and love to one another. Every single one of us. Dat is de way God plan dis world to be, and dere is no escaping it."

The cultivator blinked and drew himself up to full, drunken, argumentative height.

"Owe life to one another?" he jeered. "How dat? What dat mean?"

"Just what me say. We all owe life to one anodder, no matter how high up or low down we be in de world."

"What me owe you?" the cultivator demanded to know, swaying in his tracks. "What life me owe you? How dat can make any sense now?"

"Well," Mr. Shubert said nastily, "if you want to know, you owe me money ... dat's down in de book. But dat not what me mean."

"Lie!" the cultivator bellowed. "You only bring up dis argument so you can tell people here dat me owe you money and shame me! Dat's de only reason. Me know how shopkeeper brain work, you know, sah!"

Wounded at this suggestion, Mr. Shubert glared at the man.

"I should'a know better dan try and explain anything deep to ole negar," he said peevishly.

"Deep!" the drunken cultivator guffawed. "Dat me owe money to you shop? What deep 'bout dat? What so deep?"

A few of the onlookers jumped into the fray and a spirited argument raged. Mr. Shubert attended his exercise book and paid it no mind.

He knew his people too well: once ole negar got started on a point only Almighty God knew when he would stop.